Your Guide to Passing the PSM I Assessment

Your Guide to Passing the PSM I ASSESSMENT

Compliant with the Scrum Guide 2020

EMMA KEY

ISBN: 978-0-6489908-0-2

DISCLAIMER

This book is dedicated to my glamorous grandmother, Louise Lyddon. 2020 was a crazy year, but you didn't let that stop you from encouraging me to write this book, not once.

Contents

About the Author

Emma Key has worked for the past ten years in various roles across different industries as a Business Analyst, Customer Experience Manager, Project Manager, Scrum Master, Agile Coach and as an Agile Trainer, but her most fulfilling role is the one she's performing now - writing.

In addition to her practical, hands-on experience with Scrum, she has trained with both the Scrum Alliance and Scrum.org and achieved various certifications, including her Professional Scrum Master - Level 1 (PSM I), with Scrum.org.

Originally from Dorset in England, Emma is now living her dream in Queensland, Australia with her husband and their two children, Isabella and Hugo.

Emma's passion is helping organisations, leaders and teams' transition to an Agile mindset whilst working with them to redefine their company culture to create healthy, happy and high-performing teams.

The PSM I exam is exhaustive and rigorous; preparation will be required to achieve a passing score.

-SCRUM.ORG

Foreword

So you want to be a Scrum Master? There's no better time! As we have seen from recent events there are countries and companies that have handled change, complexity and uncertainty much better than others. The world needs great leaders and this book will help you start on this important learning journey of commitment, courage, focus, openness and respect. Who knows where it will end!

Scrum matters. Agile matters. Therefore, being great at Scrum really does matter and as a result so does the Scrum Master learning journey including this book. Scrum Masters are not just there to support teams, a great Scrum Master plays an important role in helping to bring about wider organisational change, mentor others and contribute to the wider Agile community.

Scrum celebrated 25 years in 2020 when much of the world was in the midst of a pandemic. The companies and countries which embraced the values of leadership compatible with Scrum, tended to deal with the crisis better than those who chose to live by stumbling from one crisis to the next. Leadership is a lot more than process; it is about people, trust and effective purposeful collaboration. The values of Scrum matter as part of being a leader and this goes well beyond a Scrum Team.

Scrum had its origins in software development however is now widely used in many domains and is now also applied to management, whole companies and across many industries. Scrum is particularly suited to complex problems where rapid feedback loops are necessary and where the organisation is prepared to accept the findings from empiricism rather than following a plan. The consequences of not embracing complexity are no longer just about unhappy customers, doing the wrong thing for too long can lead to disastrous consequences ranging from companies going out of business to governmental failure.

20 years have also passed since the founders of Scrum were two of the seventeen authors of the Agile manifesto in 2001. As we reflect on Agile's journey of adaption in the last 20 years we also reflect on how it could adapt and grow to the challenges that lay ahead in our complex world. According to the 14th State of Agile report, Scrum or hybrid practices including Scrum account for over 75% of respondents and SAFe as most popular scaled approach with Scrum as a key component of it. Scrum Masters are already in demand and with the increasing use of Agile being a great Scrum Master will matter even more in the future, which is why this book to help you on your journey is not only necessary but also timely.

It's been 10 years since I passed my PSM I at the start of my journey and certainly I would have been really grateful for this book then. The Scrum Guide 2020 edition is only 13 pages and simple to understand but is difficult to master and attempting the PSM I should not be underestimated. The difficulty of mastery underpins the need for this book to provide the clearly explained learning journey and structure to give the reader the framework for embedding the knowledge needed for the exam. Emma has extensive knowledge and experience as an Enterprise Agile Coach and Trainer and this book is the product of her knowledge, enthusiasm and desire to be the servant leader who helps others to success. I wish you well on your learning journey - teams, organisations and wider society will need great servant leaders as never before.

Craig Cockburn

PSM AND ENTERPRISE AGILE COACH,
EDINBURGH, SCOTLAND. JANUARY 2021

Preface

Origins of this book

My grandfather was a poet and it was no surprise that writing would become a passion of mine. As an Agile Trainer, I am frequently asked to recommend a reference book for guiding people through the PSM I assessment; one that provides a comprehensive overview of the common pitfalls and challenges people face when they take the exam.

I could not find a single book that gave a complete overview of the PSM process. I would instead find myself recommending several different books and websites because there simply wasn't one book that encompassed everything, from start to finish – from understanding what the assessment actually is to the steps you need to take to pass the exam. Since I couldn't find a book that didn't exist, I decided to write this book, to act as a single, standalone resource that covers everything from preparing for the PSM I assessment through to what you should do once you've passed.

Introduction

This book is your easy-to-read, comprehensive guide to passing the Professional Scrum Master - Level 1 (PSM I) assessment with Scrum.org. The assessment is well-known throughout the industry for being the most challenging entry-level Scrum Master certification on the market. Preparation is therefore key to passing the exam. There are no shortcuts to success!

There are three different Professional Scrum Master certification levels offered by Scrum.org:

- PSM I
- PSM II
- PSM III

This book focusses on preparing you to pass the PSM I assessment, although it does briefly touch on the differences between the three different PSM certification levels in Part 1.

Unlike a few other Scrum Master certifications, which are *hard to fail*, the PSM I is intentionally very *hard to pass*.

There are 80 multiple-choice questions that must be answered within a 60-minute timebox to achieve a minimum passing score of 85%. This only leaves room for 12 incorrect answers.

Candidates often underestimate the complexity and depth of the questions. You may be asking yourself why Scrum.org made the assessment as challenging as they have, especially considering it's an entry-level examination. It's because there are no prerequisites for taking the exam; Scrum.org wanted a way to ensure that those who passed the assessment did so because of their superior knowledge of Scrum, and not by chance, hence its level of difficulty.

Since launching in 2009, Scrum.org has issued over 516,500 Professional Scrum certifications globally, with over 376,534 of these being awarded specifically to those who have passed the PSM I assessment (based on data taken from Scrum.org's website, April 2021).

On average, 25,000 PSM I certifications are issued annually. When you compare this number against other entry-level Scrum Master certifications available on the market, such as the Certified Scrum Master (CSM) certification offered through the Scrum Alliance (averaging 45,000 certifications per year) the number of certification holders with Scrum.org may serve as an indication of the level of difficulty. However, you could equally argue that the CSM was created back in 2002, some eight years prior to the PSM I and that the number of CSM certifications awarded to date is therefore reflective of this and the Scrum Alliance being first to market with a Scrum Master certification.

Today, more and more organisations are adopting Scrum and many recruiters, hiring managers, and even Scrum Team members are themselves now using the assessment as a way to screen out prospective Scrum Masters who want to join a new Scrum Team.

Having a baseline understanding of Scrum that aligns with the latest Scrum Guide™ is only half the formula for PSM I success. You can be an expert on the Scrum framework and know absolutely everything that there is to know about Scrum, but under the pressure of taking the assessment, you may still make a handful of mistakes that cause you to fail the exam. Rest assured, Part 8 (Tips & Ticks) should help eliminate some of these common mistakes.

This book does not seek to provide you with an adequate background or a complete description of the Scrum framework; it assumes you already understand Agile and Scrum at a basic level from your experience in the field as a Scrum Master. Instead, this book aims to equip you with the tools and strategies needed to handle the ambiguity, uncertainty, and complexity of the PSM I assessment.

Intended audience

This book assumes that you are familiar with the Agile manifesto and the Agile mindset and how the Scrum framework relates to both of these. It also assumes that you have done your own research on all of the different Scrum Master certification options available (although I do briefly touch on these in Part 9), to reinforce your decision to take the PSM I assessment.

The people who will benefit most from reading this book are those who already possess a good grasp of the Scrum Master role and have at least one year's experience of acting in the capacity of a Scrum Master, serving and coaching teams and organisations on Scrum.

The content of this book is designed to be useful both to Scrum Masters who have read other books that cover an element of the PSM I, as well as those who are discovering the PSM I assessment for the very first time.

How to use this book

This book is divided into 14 parts, each one covering a key area of the assessment.

Part 1 begins with a broad introduction to the PSM I and then moves on to a number of different topics, each one challenging your knowledge and understanding about taking the assessment.

This book includes a Practice PSM I Assessment so you can test your readiness for the exam and concludes with some suggestions for what you should do once you've officially passed.

If you're interested in a specific topic, simply refer to that topic, but you will still need to have read and absorbed all the information in these pages to successfully pass the PSM I assessment. It's not meant to be read straight through, like a novel or a class curriculum. This is meant to be an active reference—a book you can flip through to find useful guidance on specific topics.

Let's get started

As the author of this book and a certified Professional Scrum Master - Level 1, I have compiled the necessary information to help you achieve your goal of passing the PSM I assessment into one single, concise resource.

Passing the PSM I was not easy. Even with my many years of experience of performing the role of a Scrum Master, I found there were still gaps in my knowledge when I came to prepare for the assessment. I discovered that I'd picked up bad habits from other Scrum Masters and misinterpreted the Scrum Guide™. This book consolidates everything that I have learned along the way to successfully pass the exam, so I am confident that this book will do the same for you, too.

PART 1
About the PSM

There is a well-known Chinese proverb that says, "A journey of a thousand miles starts beneath one's feet". I would like to congratulate you on taking your first step towards PSM I certification.

This section of the book aims to provide you with a gentle introduction to the PSM I. It covers the assessment syllabus, and gives you a solid understanding of the different PSM certification options available from Scrum.org, and how they are related.

1

Origins of the Scrum Master

The role of the Scrum Master can be traced back nearly 30 years, to the time when Jeff Sutherland, John Scrumniotales and Jeff McKenna started to implement elements of what we know today as the Scrum framework, at the Easel Corporation, in 1993. They took their inspiration from the book, *Wicked Problems, Righteous Solutions* (DeGrace and Stahl, 1990), which explained why the traditional Waterfall approach to software development no longer worked; DeGrace and Stahl showed that the user only really knows what they want after they see an initial version of the software or product.

However, it wasn't until five years later, in 1998, that the term Scrum Master was officially coined in a white paper titled *SCRUM: An extension pattern language for hyperproductive software development*. Up until this point, the Scrum Master role did not exist. In 2001, following the publication of Ken Schwaber and Mike Beedle's book, *Agile Software Development with Scrum*, the idea of the Scrum Master began to develop towards the role described in the 2010 version of *The Scrum Guide™* (2010); the opening paragraph of the guide explains that, 'The Scrum Master is responsible for the success of Scrum [...]. The Scrum Master is responsible for ensuring that Scrum values, practices and rules are enacted and enforced.' The Scrum Master role described here has evolved a lot since then - and for the better!

Since 2001, many of the Scrum Master's accountabilities described in the book are now shared across the entire Scrum Team rather than being exclusively led or driven by the Scrum Master. The role of the Scrum Master has, in fact, changed significantly over the years compared to other roles on the Scrum Team (e.g. Product Owner and the Developers). The supportive 21st Century Scrum Master that you know today first started to really come into being in 2010, with the first edition of *The Scrum Guide™*.

The terms 'ScrumMaster' and 'Scrum Master' are used interchangeably and there is no clear industry standard for the correct title. The Scrum Alliance use the term ScrumMaster (one word), whereas Scrum.org use the term Scrum Master (two words). However, the Scrum Guide™ (which we'll come to later) uses the term Scrum Master.

Further Reading

Mike Beedle, Martine Devos, Yonat Sharon, Ken Schwaber, Jeff Sutherland (1998): *SCRUM: An extension pattern language for hyperproductive software development.*

Ken Schwaber, Mike Beedle (2001): *Agile Software Development with Scrum.*

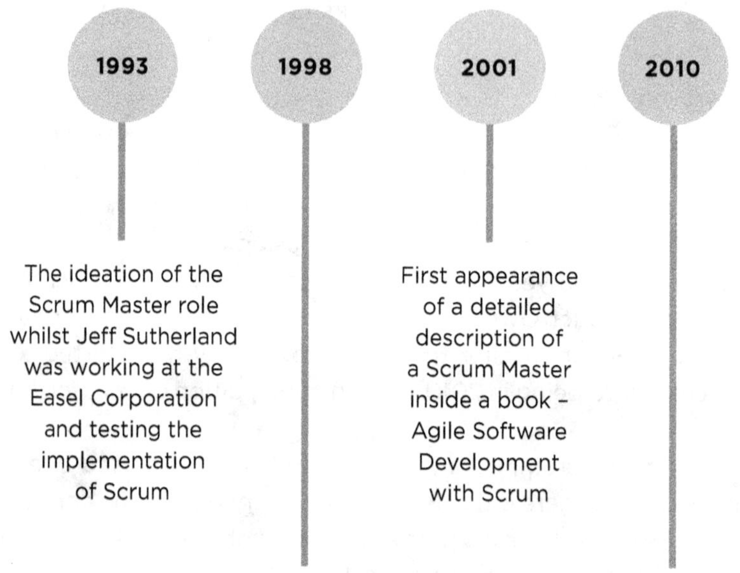

Figure 1.1 Origins of the Scrum Master

2

Importance of the Scrum Master

The term *Scrum Master* was initially used to indicate someone who is an expert at Scrum.

Having a skilled and experienced Scrum Master on a Scrum Team is not optional; the Scrum Team's success depends on it! The role of the Scrum Master is vital; the person in the role is responsible for overseeing the optimal implementation of the Scrum framework. They do this by helping everyone on the Scrum Team and in the wider organisation to understand Scrum theory, practice, rules, and values.

Unfortunately, not every organisation sees the value in having a Scrum Master. Sometimes, at the Executive level, people question whether the work of a Scrum Master actually consumes 100% of their time. In fact, some organisations that adopt Scrum decide not to hire a Scrum Master at all. The organisations that take this route incorrectly see the Scrum Master as just a facilitator; they assume that someone either inside or outside the Scrum Team will be able to step in and step out of the role as the organisation sees fit. This is a mistake; to put it simply, it is not possible to realise the full benefits of the Scrum framework without hiring a Scrum Master. Think about a basketball team without a Coach; the team would be less likely to reach their full potential. As we see in sport, teams that have a Coach onboard tend to perform better, learn quicker and have a wider range of experience to draw upon and improve.

In some organisations, the Scrum Master role is combined with the role of a Developer, which is in-line with the latest version of the Scrum Guide™. As a result, and speaking from personal experience, Scrum Masters can find it challenging to decide which role takes precedence and, more often than not, they tend to default to the role that is more visible, such as that of a Developer. The Scrum Master can even lead several Scrum Teams concurrently. Again, the Scrum Guide™ doesn't explicitly state that the Scrum Master can't servant-lead more than one Scrum Team. However, numerous studies have shown that the productivity of Scrum Teams, especially teams less experienced in the implementation of Scrum, increases dramatically when they have a dedicated Scrum Master on board.

3

Future of the Scrum Master

With the Scrum framework fast becoming standard practice worldwide in most organisations using Agile, Scrum Masters are in great demand. A *2019 report* published by Scrum.org and Age of Product, concluded that the Scrum Master role was:

- growing in use and importance, with 81% of organisations using Scrum;
- seeing an increase in higher salaries for those who hold a Scrum Master certification;
- driving change at the enterprise level;
- seeing growth in terms of salaries as the role matures in organisations;
- closing the gender gap for salaries between men and women.

The Scrum Master role made it onto LinkedIn's list of the 'Most Promising Jobs for 2019'. It was placed #10 out of a total of #15 most promising jobs for 2019. According to LinkedIn, this increased demand has given the role a median base salary of $103,000 US Dollars and a year-on-year predicted job growth of 67%, which will likely drive base salaries even higher as demand for the role continues to increase.

The Scrum Master role has changed a lot since the late 1990s and is likely to continue to develop and evolve over the next few years, especially following the changes made to the latest version of the Scrum Guide™ (2020).

Further Reading

Scrum.org, Age of Product (2019): *The Scrum Master Trends Report.*

LinkedIn (2019): *Most Promising Jobs.*

4

The PSM

The acronym *PSM* stands for 'Professional Scrum Master' and is a registered trademark of Scrum.org: Scrum.org Professional Scrum Master™ I (PSM I™).

Traditionally, a Scrum Master is someone who is accountable for establishing Scrum as defined in the Scrum Guide™, whereas a *Professional* Scrum Master is a Scrum Master who has achieved his or her Professional Scrum Master designation through Scrum.org, having demonstrated their exceptional knowledge and understanding of Scrum and their ability to apply it in real-world situations. Essentially, the difference between a Scrum Master and a Professional Scrum Master is the award of the PSM certification from Scrum.org.

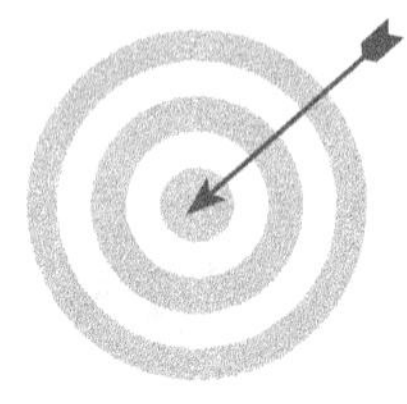

5

Levels of Accreditation

Recognised globally throughout the industry, Scrum.org offers three levels of Professional Scrum Master accreditations:

- PSM I
- PSM II
- PSM III

The PSM family of assessments covers a range of areas related to the knowledge and real-world implementation of Scrum. PSM I is considered the entry-level certification, PSM II the practitioner-level certification and PSM III the expert-level certification.

All three assessments are available online only and need to be taken consecutively. That is to say, obtaining your PSM I certification is a prerequisite for taking the PSM II assessment and likewise, the PSM II certification is a prerequisite for taking the PSM III assessment. There are currently no prerequisites for taking the PSM I exam.

For a long time, recertification could be added to the short list of certainties in life, like death and taxes. However, this changed a few years ago, so that now when you receive an accreditation from Scrum.org, it does not expire and you do not need to update it to retain your certification status – it has lifetime validity. Scrum.

org are leading the way with lifetime certifications, with other industry organisations (such as Microsoft) now adopting the same approach. It means you could return to work from an extended career break and not have to resit the PSM I before progressing onto the PSM II, saving you both time and money.

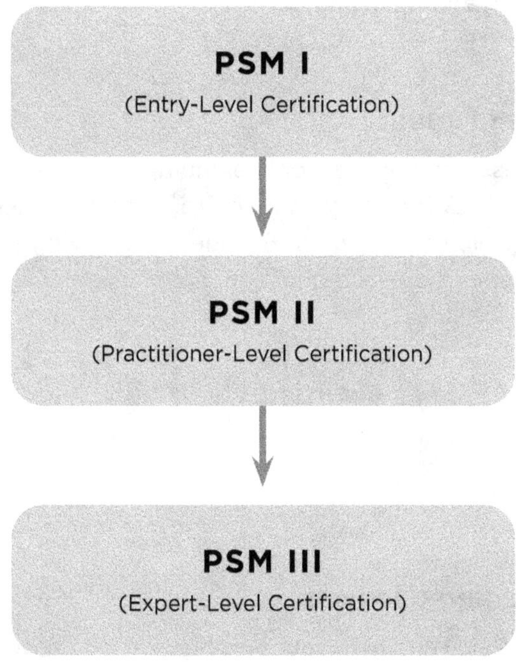

Figure 1.2 Professional Scrum Master Certification Levels

The PSM I

The Professional Scrum Master – Level I (PSM I) is the foundation-level Scrum Master certification available through Scrum.org. Although it's the foundation-level certification, it's renowned for being the most challenging out of all the entry-level Scrum Master certifications available; hence why it has a difficulty rating of 'intermediate'. Those who pass the assessment receive the industry recognised PSM I certification to demonstrate their mastery of Scrum.

PSM I validates your knowledge of the Scrum framework, which is key to success in any role on a Scrum Team. The assessment questions are primarily about the Scrum framework, rules, and values. Certificate holders prove that they understand Scrum as described in the Scrum Guide™ and how to apply those concepts in real-world situations. They also have a consistent approach to implementing and following Scrum.

Assessment Format

The PSM I assessment is an online, multiple-choice exam. Some questions will ask for one or more correct answers. You'll have 60 minutes in which to complete 80 questions, giving you only 45 seconds to spend on each question.

Number of PSM I's Awarded

At the time of writing, 376,534 PSM I certifications have been awarded.

What is Required to Pass

To pass the PSM I and gain your certification, you have to achieve a pass score of at least 85%. This means you need to understand the Scrum framework extremely well and have experience as a Scrum Master and/or an understanding of how to be effective in the role. However, those who are planning ahead and considering becoming a Professional Scrum Trainer (PST) with Scrum.org will need to achieve a pass score of at least 95% on the PSM I, as this is a prerequisite to progress onto the PST certification programme.

The Cost

Currently, the cost of taking the assessment is $150[1] US Dollars for a single attempt.

The PSM II

The Professional Scrum Master - Level 2 (PSM II) is the advanced-level Scrum Master certification available through Scrum.org. It is a practitioner-level test designed to gauge your understanding of how to actually apply the Scrum principles in a practical sense during challenging situations that may be experienced by Scrum Teams, projects, and anyone else within your organisation. It follows on from the theory side of the PSM I exam into the practical application of Scrum.

The assessment is exhaustive and rigorous. The questions are designed to make you think about and interpret the concepts in the Scrum Guide™, and apply content from PSM II subject areas; you will also need to refer to your own experience as a Scrum Master.

Assessment Format

The exam consists of 30 questions, some true-false, some multiple-choice, and some multiple-answer, and you have 90 minutes in which to complete the test. Some questions are worth 1 point, some 2 and some 3. There are some questions (multiple-answer questions) that award partial marks if part of the answer is correct.

Number of PSM II's Awarded

At the time of writing, 11,286 PSM II certifications have been awarded.

---

1 Please refer to Scrum.org's website for the latest pricing.

What is Required to Pass

To pass the PSM II, you have to achieve a pass score of at least 85%. The questions are almost all based on challenging situations where you need to evaluate what is going on in the scenario, determine possible courses of action based on the rules, principles, and values of Scrum, and understand the potential ramifications of those actions. You need to know the Scrum framework exceedingly well, and have concrete experience as a Scrum Master in similar situations.

The Cost

Currently, the cost of taking the assessment is $250[2] US Dollars for a single attempt.

The PSM III

The Professional Scrum Master - Level 3 (PSM III) is the highest level of Professional Scrum Master certification available through Scrum.org and it represents 'a distinguished level of Scrum Mastery'. Originally, this exam was called the PSM II but was re-branded as the PSM III in July 2016.

The PSM III assessment is an extremely challenging essay-based exam designed to determine an individual's effectiveness in the capacity of a trainer and as a coach of the Scrum framework.

Assessment Format

To pass the PSM III, you have to achieve a score of at least 85% within the 150-minute timebox. There are a total of 30 questions,

---

2 Please refer to Scrum.org's website for the latest pricing.

which are a combination of essay and multiple-choice answers. However, those who are considering becoming a Professional Scrum Trainer (PST) with Scrum.org need to achieve a score of at least 95% on the PSM III, as this is a prerequisite to progressing to the PST certification programme.

Number of PSM III's Awarded

At the time of writing, 952 PSM III certifications have been awarded.

What is Required to Pass

To pass the PSM III, you need to know the Scrum framework inside and out, and also have built-up a significant amount of experience as a Scrum Master, a Scrum Coach and as a Scrum Trainer, in order to draw on your experience.

It is recommended that before someone takes the PSM III exam, they should have had at least three years' experience as a Scrum Master, taken a PSM training course to make sure they fully understand the Scrum terminology, and have had a significant amount of experience in creating and conducting training on Scrum and Agile topics.

The Cost

Currently, the cost of the assessment is $500[3] US Dollars for a single attempt.

---

3 Please refer to Scrum.org's website for the latest pricing.

Certification Criteria	PSM I	PSM II	PSM III
Number of Questions	x 80	x 30	x 30
Pass Mark Questions	68 questions answered correctly	25.5 questions answered correctly	25.5 questions answered correctly
Pass Mark Percentage	85%	85%	85%
Exam Duration	60 minutes	90 minutes	150 minutes
Required Course Attendance	Optional	Optional	Optional
Perceived Difficulty Level	Intermediate	Advanced	Expert
Certification Expiry	Lifetime Validity	Lifetime Validity	Lifetime Validity
Cost	*$150 US Dollars	*$250 US Dollars	*$500 US Dollars
Language	English	English	English
Exam Format	Multiple Choice, Multiple Answer and True/ False	Multiple Choice, Multiple Answer and True/ False	Multiple Choice and Essay

**Subject to change.*

Figure 1.3 Professional Scrum Master Certification Comparison Table

6

PSM I Assessment Syllabus

Scrum.org has created a set of five *Professional Scrum Competencies* to guide individuals on their professional development journey with Scrum. The exam syllabus for the PSM I is based on a subset of these competencies, four to be exact.

The PSM I assessment is the formal process of collecting evidence of the required competencies (skills and knowledge) gained through your understanding and application of Scrum.

Each professional Scrum competency contains a number of key areas, which provide the finer detail of the desired knowledge, skills, and behaviours that you need to have in order to master a specific competency.

The professional Scrum competencies and associated focus areas apply to the entire Scrum Team which is made up of one Scrum Master, one Product Owner and the Developers.

If you are planning to attend a PSM I training course with a certified Professional Scrum Trainer, the training materials and training syllabus will be aligned with the four core professional Scrum competencies listed in Figure 1.4.

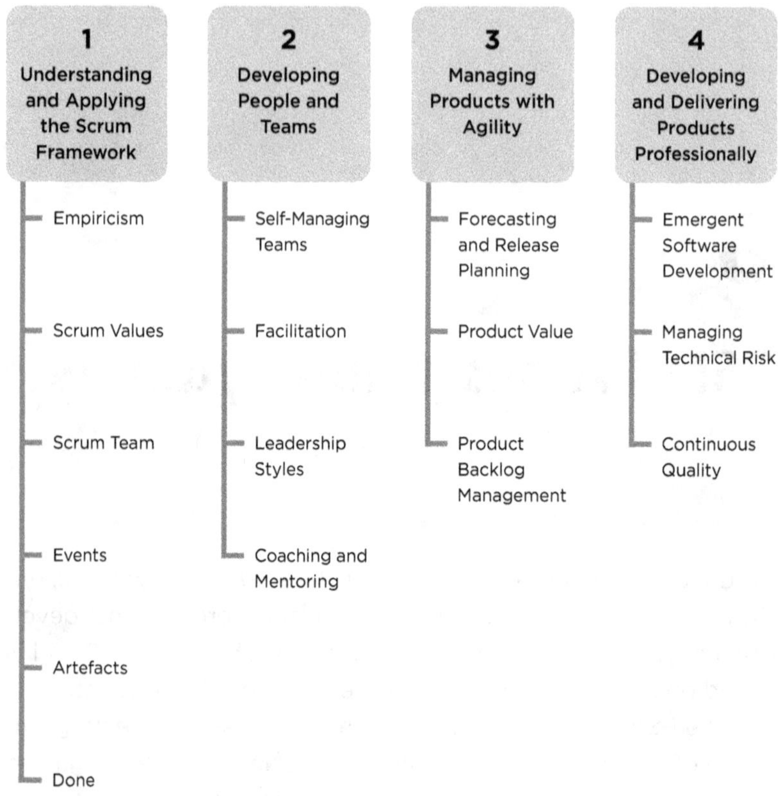

Figure 1.4 The 4 Professional Scrum Competencies of the PSM I

PSM I Syllabus

The PSM I assessment focusses on four of the five Professional Scrum Competencies:

1 **Understanding and Applying the Scrum Framework:** Focus Areas: Empiricism, Scrum Values, Scrum Team, Events, Artefacts, Done.

2 **Developing People and Teams:**
Focus Areas: Self-Managing Teams, Facilitation, Leadership Styles, Coaching and Mentoring.

3 **Managing Products with Agility:**
Focus Areas: Forecasting and Release Planning, Product Value, Product Backlog Management

4 **Developing and Delivering Products Professionally:**
Focus Areas: Emergent Software Development, Managing Technical Risk, Continuous Quality

Scrum.org does not share the weightings for each professional Scrum competency and associated focus areas, but instead recommends that candidates invest their efforts on fostering a more complete understanding of the Scrum practices and mindset, rather than looking for the quickest route to passing the PSM I assessment.

During the PSM I assessment, questions are randomly generated. It is also not explicitly stated which question relates to which of the four PSM I competencies in figure 1.4.

Understanding and Applying the Scrum Framework

The Scrum framework is a structure that helps and supports Scrum Teams to work together. In rugby, a *Scrum* moves as a cohesive unit working towards a common goal, reflecting along the way on what's propelling them forward and what's holding them back from reaching their optimum performance levels.

Within the 'Understanding and Applying the Scrum Framework' Professional Scrum Competency, there are six areas of focus, as depicted in Figure 1.5 on the next page.

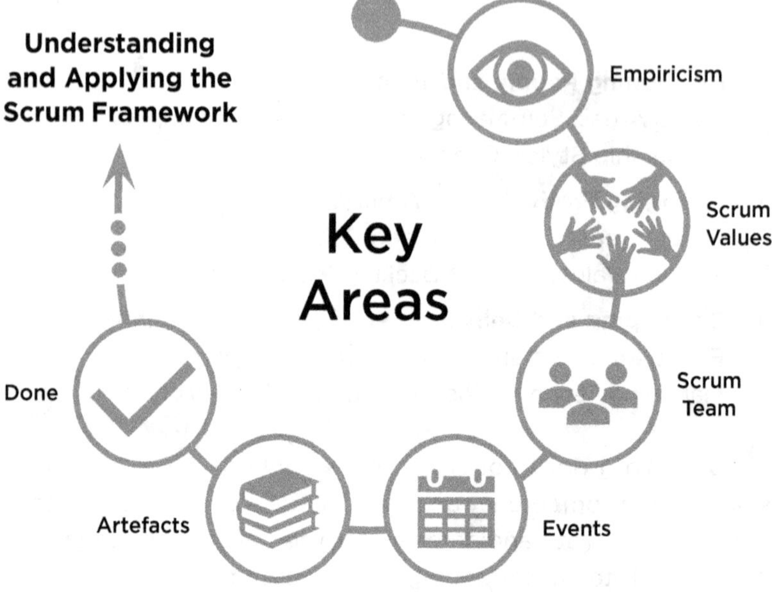

Figure 1.5 Competency: Understanding and Applying the Scrum Framework

Empiricism

Scrum is based on the empirical process. Empiricism is the act of making decisions based on what is actually known from our experiences. Scrum is built upon the three pillars of empiricism - Transparency, Inspection and Adaptation. If these three pillars aren't upheld the whole Scrum framework is unsupported and at risk of collapse. For the PSM I, you are required to understand what empiricism is and how it fits into the mechanics of Scrum.

Scrum Team

As mentioned, a Scrum Team consists of one Scrum Master, one Product Owner and the Developers. Each of the three accountabilities has a very clear set of responsibilities. Together, these three accountabilities form the *Scrum Team*. To pass the PSM I, you will need to understand what is required of each of these accountabilities, how they differ from one another and the implications of these with Human Resources as they are applied to more traditional roles within your organisation.

Scrum Values

Success with Scrum depends on the entire Scrum Team embodying five core values: commitment, courage, focus, openness, and respect. These values give direction to the work, behaviour and actions in Scrum. Values drive behaviour. A competent Professional Scrum Master will understand the Scrum Values in-depth, and be able to draw on their experience of applying them in organisations whose values do not necessarily align with those of Scrum.

Events

The Scrum framework contains five events: The Sprint, Sprint Planning, Daily Scrum, Sprint Review, and the Sprint Retrospective. All events are timeboxed and enable progress through empiricism. For the assessment, you will need to have extensive knowledge and experience of practical application of these events in challenging situations, and with teams using scaled Scrum.

Artefacts

The Scrum framework confirms three artefacts; the Product Backlog, Sprint Backlog, and the Increment. These artefacts are considered to be the absolute minimum in terms of the tools needed to successfully plan, execute, and review the progress of the Sprint. You will need to understand the purpose of these artefacts and how to apply them practically alongside an organisation's existing tools.

'Done'

The Definition of Done is essentially a list of acceptance criteria that is applied to every item on the Sprint Backlog, in order for the Scrum Team to deliver what it considers to be a 'Done' product Increment during the Sprint. The moment a Product Backlog item meets the Definition of Done, an Increment is created. As part of the assessment, you will be expected to describe what the Definition of Done is and how it is best communicated within an organisation.

Developing People and Teams

Once the Scrum Team is in place, it's important to remember that these teams are like individuals; they require leadership, mentoring, coaching and space to self-manage in order to continuously develop and grow together.

Unlocking the potential of individuals in teams is fundamental for an Agile culture to truly flourish. Scrum Teams need to be given the knowledge and mechanisms to create a healthy foundation on which Agile initiatives can succeed and complex challenges can be solved.

Within the 'Developing People and Teams' professional Scrum competency, there are four areas of focus, as depicted in Figure 1.6 below.

Coaching, Mentoring and *Facilitation* are proven to be effective approaches to fostering team collaboration and *self-managing teams*. To build and maintain an Agile culture, Scrum Masters need to align the behaviours of Scrum Teams, as well as those in the rest of the organisation, with the Agile principles and Scrum values, making *Leadership* a crucial competency for Scrum Masters to drive change.

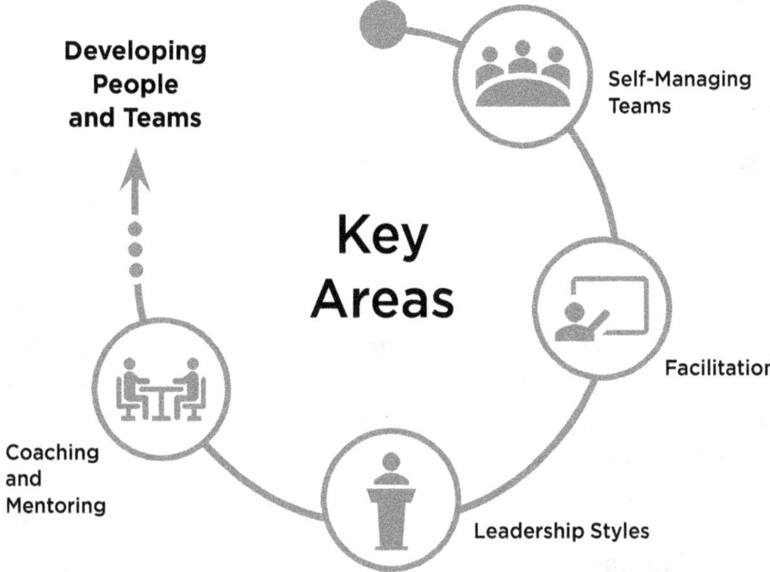

Figure 1.6 Competency: Developing People and Teams

Self-Managing Teams

One of the twelve principles from the Agile Manifesto states, "the best architectures, requirements, and designs emerge from self-organising teams." Self-managing teams choose how best to accomplish their work, instead of being directed by others outside the Scrum Team. You will need to have knowledge of what a self-managing team is and the signs to look out for to determine if a team is self-managing or not and the methods for leading a team to become self-managing, such as problem-solving techniques.

Facilitation

Being a good facilitator is a fundamental skill of a Professional Scrum Master, as you will need to facilitate stakeholder collaboration when needed. It is therefore essential that you understand the benefits of facilitation and have a range of experience in applying different facilitation tools in varying contexts.

Leadership Styles

The Scrum Master is described in the Scrum Guide™ as being a 'true leader' whose focus should be on both the needs of the Scrum Team and the larger organisation. However, being a great leader alone is not enough to be successful in your role and you should look to master several different leadership styles to support each unique Scrum Team and organisation that you encounter. There are many different styles of leadership; having a toolbox of these styles and a clear idea of when to use each one will serve you well in the assessment.

Coaching and Mentoring

A Scrum Master is a trainer, mentor and coach. Coaching is about unlocking a team's potential with a view to maximising their performance. You will need to understand the benefits of coaching and have experience in applying your coaching skills to different situations. As a mentor, you will draw on your Scrum Master experience to help guide the Scrum Team through the challenge they are facing.

Managing Products with Agility

In Agile product development, product management is based upon guiding a product through multiple iterations. This approach is more fluid than other more traditional product development approaches and gives more flexibility to the product being developed.

Within the 'Managing Products with Agility' professional Scrum competency, there are three areas of focus, as depicted in Figure 1.7 below.

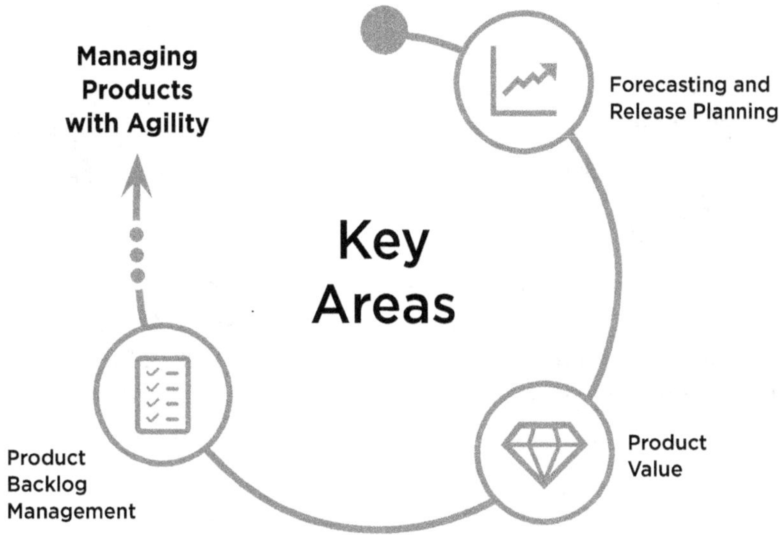

Figure 1.7 Competency: Managing Products with Agility

Forecasting and Release Planning

During a Sprint, the Scrum Team will strive to produce a potentially releasable Increment of value and use to the customer. A release plan looks at when a coherent set of items, from across one Sprint or more, will be ready for release to the customer. If required by the Scrum Team, the Scrum Master facilitates a session to help the team to work out when releases will happen. For the PSM I assessment, you will need knowledge and experience of applying different Sprint forecasting and release planning techniques.

Product Value

The purpose of a Scrum Team is to ultimately deliver the Product Goal and to optimise the delivery of the goal in the most efficient and effective way through the use of the Scrum Values. Customer value should be the driving factor behind the Product Goal. At the PSM I level, you should be able to use a range of different approaches for defining, communicating and measuring value to assist the Scrum Team and the organisation.

Product Backlog Management

The Product Backlog is a prioritised list of items for the Developers to turn into an Increment of the product. It is continuously maintained by either the Product Owner or a person of their choosing so that the highest-value items are at the top of the backlog so that the Scrum Team knows which items to select from the list first. As a minimum, you should know what a Product Backlog is, the purpose that it serves and be familiar with a number of techniques for managing it.

Developing and Delivering Products Professionally

Throughout my career as a Scrum Master, I have found there to be a common misconception that, in Scrum practice, quality is traded for speed. When implemented properly, Scrum leads to higher-quality products being delivered faster than using more traditional product delivery methods. Speed is a by-product of Scrum Teams working more efficiently and removing impediments.

Within the 'Developing and Delivering Products Professionally' professional Scrum competency, there are three areas of focus, as depicted in Figure 1.8 below.

Delivering high-quality products can be achieved by building the product in a series of iterations and frequently putting the product in the hands of the customer for continuous feedback, ensuring the end product delivered is exactly what the customer is expecting - without any unwelcomed surprises!

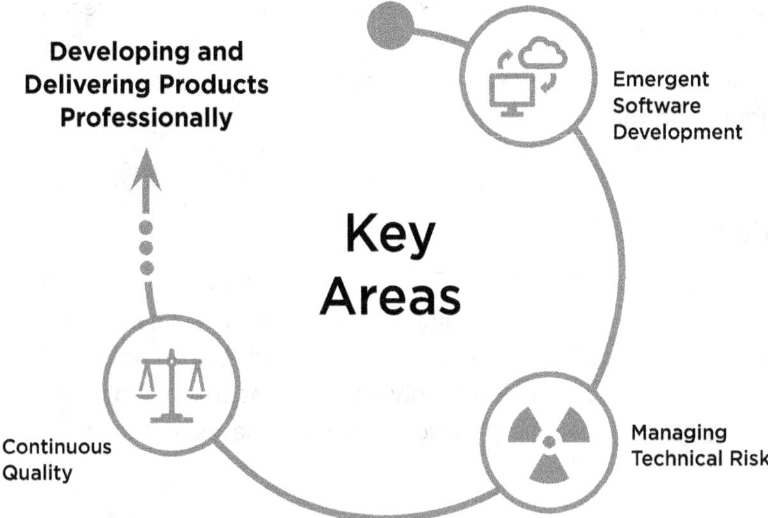

Figure 1.8 Competency: Developing and Delivering Products Professionally

Emergent Software Development

Scrum Teams do not do all of the analysis and design work upfront and instead start delivering working functionality and letting the design emerge over time. This is known as emergent software development. The analysis and design is done incrementally because doing it all upfront means it takes longer to get the product into the hands of the customer. As a Scrum Master, you need to know what emergent software development is, and be able to explain the value that it offers.

Managing Technical Risk

Technical risk management in Scrum is about reducing the probability and impact of adverse events around a product's delivery.

Due to its iterative nature, the Scrum framework implicitly makes risk management a part of the product delivery life cycle. As a Scrum Master, you are expected to know how to manage technical risk as part of the empirical process and how to apply effective practices to make risk management transparent to the Scrum Team and the wider organisation.

Continuous Quality

In Scrum, quality is defined as the ability to build the product Increment to meet the Definition of Done and achieve the business value expected by the customer. Scrum adopts an approach of continuous improvement involving frequent testing to optimise the probability of the product achieving the expected levels of quality.

7

History of the PSM I Assessment

The history of the PSM I assessment begins with the formation of the Scrum Alliance in 2001; Ken Schwaber was one of Scrum Alliance's founders. Ken later left the Scrum Alliance after disagreement over how decisions were made in relation to the assessment and certification process and subsequently founded Scrum.org in 2009.

Scrum.org's mission is - *to improve the profession of Software Delivery.*

The original Scrum Guide™ was co-created in 2010 by Jeff Sutherland and Ken Schwaber and is at the heart of the PSM I assessment.

The PSM I and PSM II assessments were first introduced as part of the Scrum.org certification portfolio back in 2009.

Alongside the PSM assessments, Scrum.org also released an assessment called the Professional Scrum Practitioner (PSP).

After launching the PSM assessments, Scrum.org received feedback from candidates reporting that they felt the PSM II was too difficult to pass and a too big a step up from the PSM I. Scrum.org conducted some further research into these claims and discovered that the word *practitioner* also caused some confusion.

Having identified a gap in the family of PSM assessments for an intermediary-level certification, the PSM II exam was re-branded the PSM III and the PSP was subsequently re-branded as the PSM II.

Those people who already held the PSM II were automatically re-designated as a PSM III and similarly those who had the PSP were automatically switched to having the PSM II designation.

This journey has been shaped by two opposing forces: the desire to do the right thing, and the desire to make money. I formed Scrum.org to refocus my efforts on doing the right thing.

-KEN SCHWABER FOUNDER OF SCRUM.ORG

PART 2

Understanding and Applying the Scrum Framework

As a Scrum Master your raison d'être is to enable others to master Scrum, and to help them understand the core principles and values of Scrum.

The Scrum Guide™ states that the Scrum Master is accountable for establishing Scrum as defined in the Scrum Guide™. This is achieved by the Scrum Master helping the Scrum Team and the organisation to understand and apply Scrum theory, practice, rules and values. As a Scrum Master you can only successfully achieve this if you fully understand Scrum.

You need to ensure you have a solid grasp of the Scrum framework, as well as how to best apply it in your organisation. This part of the book breaks the framework down into bite-sized chunks that you can easily digest, and highlights areas that you may have missed or overlooked on your journey to becoming a Professional Scrum Master.

8

Pillars of Empiricism

Scrum is built on the three pillars of Empiricism - transparency, inspection and adaptation. If these aren't 'upheld' the whole framework is unsupported and thus unstable.

Empirical process control (or empiricism) asserts that knowledge comes from experience, observation and experimentation. Using this principle, we can make decisions based on what is known at a given point in time. Scrum Team's need to inspect the data and make decisions about further investigation until they see the desired output. Empirical process control works well when the underlying process is inherently complex and/or the process is not well understood or is imperfectly defined. The results are not repeatable and are unpredictable. Empirical process control works through frequent inspection and adaptation.

Let's look at an example. A teashop normally serves standard green tea. To make the tea, it involves processing the input (tea bag and water) so they get the desired output (green tea) using tools (tea pot, mug, spoon) and techniques (heating the water, brewing mechanism). These processes are known, repeatable, predictable, every part of the process is understood, and the process can be started and run with the same results every single time to produce hot green tea.

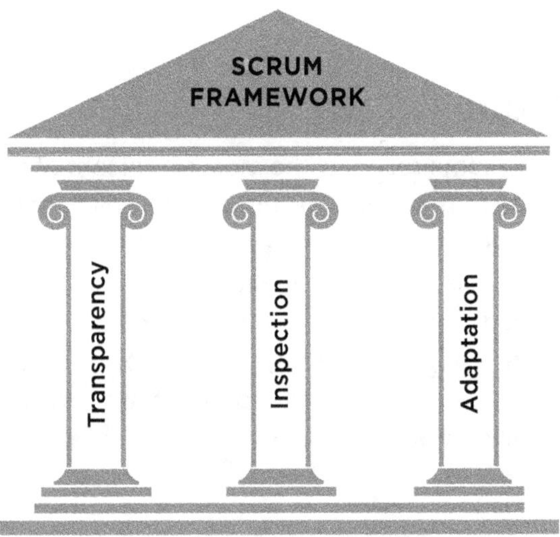

Figure 2.1 The Three Pillars of Empiricism

Let's say the same tea shop wants to start making cakes. They've never made these before, and they don't know the process to follow, let alone the required techniques and tools. This is a good example of evolutionary product planning. The only way the tea shop will be able to make cakes is through inspection and adaptation - experimenting with a new process, inspecting that process, and adapting or making changes to that process as needed, until they reach the desired result - or in this case, a delicious slice of cake!

The same applies to Scrum. In short, the Scrum Team can learn and improve upon past mistakes and experiences.

Transparency

When transparency is working well in Scrum, team members, executives, and stakeholders know what is going on with the Product at any given point in time. They have easy access to information and have solid communication channels at their disposal.

Transparency is depicted through burn-down charts, Sprint Reviews and Sprint Retrospectives, etc.

Inspection

Inspection is in some respects the most significant of the three pillars of empiricism that define a successful Scrum Team. The team must ensure that the Scrum artefacts are frequently inspected so that any unwanted variance impacting the success of the Sprint Goal is removed.

Inspection is depicted through interaction with the customer and discussing the Scrum Teams progress towards the Sprint Goal during the Daily Scrum, etc.

Adaptation

In the Waterfall process model, changes and adjustments are really difficult to make; the Scrum framework is widely used by many organisations because of its adaptability. Of course, adaptation is not possible without the first two pillars highlighted in figure 2.1. It is only when the Scrum Team practices transparency and inspection that they can figure out whether design elements have to be *adapted.* Once it is determined that adaptation is required, it is carried out as soon as possible to optimise the outcome of the Sprint.

Adaptation is depicted through the Sprint Review and the Sprint Retrospective where the team acquires feedback from the customer and also identifies what needs to change going forward.

9

The Scrum Team

Within the Scrum Framework all the work delivered to the customer is done so by the Scrum Team. A Scrum Team is a collection of individuals working together to build and deliver the product Increment.

Within the Scrum framework three accountabilities are defined:

- Scrum Master
- Product Owner
- The Developers

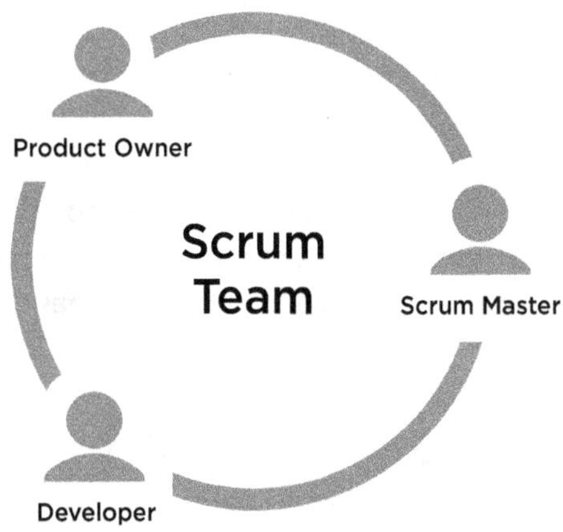

Figure 2.2 The Scrum Team

Scrum Master

As described in the Scrum Guide™, the Scrum Master is accountable for establishing Scrum within a Scrum Team and the wider-organisation. Scrum Masters do this by helping everyone understand Scrum theory, practice, rules, and values.

The Scrum Master is the person on the team who is responsible for helping the team to maximise their effectiveness: They are not involved in the decision-making, but act as a lodestar to guide the team through the Scrum process using their experience, expertise and leadership.

Not everyone on the Scrum Team will have the same understanding of Scrum, and this is especially true for teams new to the framework. Without a Scrum Master coaching the Scrum Team, and helping team members understand the theory, practice, rules and values of scrum, the project can flounder and fail - so your role as a Scrum Master is mandatory, not optional!

Product Owner

The Product Owner is primarily a 'products person'; this role is quite different from that of a Project Manager or Delivery Manager who is primarily responsible for the delivery of an outcome. The Product Owner lives and breathes the product, knows how it works, who uses it, when they use it, why they use it and most importantly, its limitations and their ramifications. They are ultimately accountable for maximising the value of the product.

The Product Owner should be able to speak with authority on any of the product features, the value these deliver and the business rules which drive them. They may need to defer detailed technical questions to the Developers, but they should have a broad understanding of the product, and changes in the market which present opportunities or challenges for product performance.

The Product Owner knows who their customers are and understands their needs and motivations; they know what is most important to them and why. Having empathy for the customer is critical for a Product Owner — it enables them to determine the value of potential new features by assessing these from the customer's perspective, and then prioritising them in the Product Backlog accordingly. The Product Owner fills a key role in defining purpose for the Developers, by describing the product vision and setting the Product Goal that they are striving towards. Essentially it is up to the Product Owner to be able to confidently answer the question: 'why are we building this?'

The Developers

As described in the Scrum Guide™, the Developers consist of professionals who do the work of delivering a potentially releasable Increment of 'Done' product during the Sprint. Only the Developers create the Increment but it is the entire Scrum Team who are accountable for ensuring it is of value and use to the customer.

The Scrum Team is a self-managing, cross-functional team of people who are collectively responsible for all of the work necessary to produce working, usable products.

There is no fixed-size for a Scrum Team, but the Scrum Guide™ makes the recommendation that it is 10 people or fewer. It may vary from one Scrum Team to another. Ideally, a Scrum Team should be small enough to remain agile and large enough to complete a significant amount of work within a specific Sprint. This will result in a product of the best possible value.

Traditional Roles

Probably one of the biggest challenge's organisations face when they make the transition to Scrum is how this fits with more traditional roles, e.g. Project Manager. How this is managed is unique to each organisation and there isn't a standard way to tackle this. As a Scrum Master, you will need to work with Human Resources to explore the best way to address this based on your experience and applying what's worked well elsewhere in other organisations.

10

Scrum Values

All of Scrum's principles and processes are built upon five values known aptly as the Scrum Values -Commitment, Focus, Openness, Respect and Courage. When these values are adhered to fervently by the Scrum Team, the three Scrum pillars of transparency, inspection, and adaptation are upheld and the Scrum framework supported. The Scrum Values help to guide Scrum Teams to self-manage and know the right thing to do in the event they become stuck; they act as a compass to drive the right behaviours.

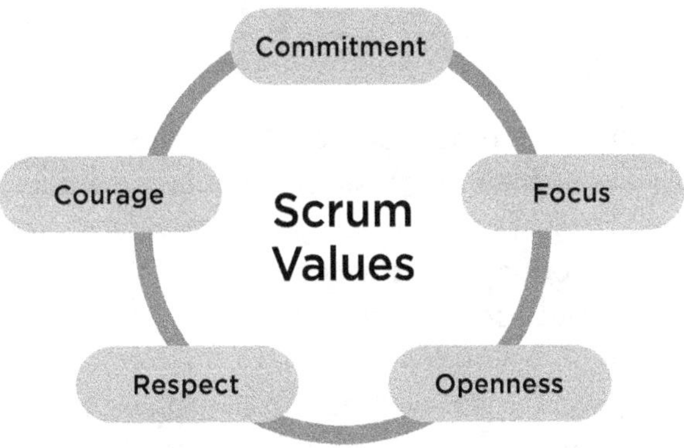

Figure 2.3 The Five Scrum Values

Commitment

Without each member's commitment, Scrum Teams will struggle to learn, collaborate and, ultimately, deliver product Increments on time. Unless everyone on the Scrum Team commits fully to the same Sprint Goal and working in the same direction, it won't be possible to work fast and adapt. Scrum Team members must own up to their commitments and do what they say they are going to do. It's also equally as important not to overcommit, or take on more than you conceivably can, as this will affect the rest of your team.

Focus

Complexity and uncertainty are two staples of the product development landscape. It's important that Scrum Teams maintain a clear product vision and stay laser-focused as user needs and priorities shift. Think of it this way. If there are 100 things to do, would you rather do 10 of them well, or all 100 passably? Even with the best-laid Sprint plans, Scrum Teams can quickly feel overloaded.

While these values may seem like common sense, they are critical in implementing Scrum successfully.

Openness

To inspect and adapt products and processes, Scrum Teams need to be open about their progress. Scrum Team members need to feel comfortable sharing their work and raising issues about what's coming next. Product Owners need to be able to provide and accept honest feedback. As the Scrum Master, you can assist the Scrum Team by creating trusting working relationships between the Product Owner, the Developers and business stakeholders.

Respect

Everyone is coming from a different place in life, and they bring different experiences and identities with them. To work as a Scrum Team, they need to respect each other's differences. Better still, they should celebrate them!

Let's take the Developers for example. These are a group of cross-functional individuals. They may not share skillsets, but they do need to work in concert. Each person has to assume that others have good intentions and respect that they are doing their best to reach the same Sprint Goal.

Courage

People outside the Scrum Team can't necessarily gauge the team's progress, yet they depend on the team to produce vital product Increments. The entire company relies on them to be honest about their work and the challenges they face. This requires courage at every turn. Scrum Team members must have the courage to tell the truth and to speak the truth to the Product Owner and even those outside of the Scrum Team, such as business stakeholders. It's not easy to tell the organisation that what they are doing isn't in the best interests of the customer and to insist that it needs changing; this requires courage.

In my experience as a Scrum Master, one of the best ways you can assist the Scrum Team with adhering to the five Scrum Values is simply leading by example.

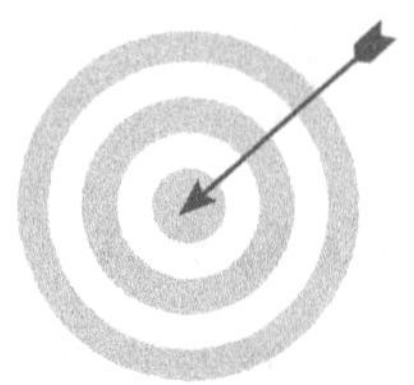

11

Scrum Events

There are technically five events in Scrum. The Sprint itself is classed as an event and acts as a container for all of the other Scrum events. You'd be mistaken for thinking these events are optional as failure to incorporate any event as part of the Sprint results in lost opportunities for the Scrum Team to inspect and adapt and ultimately reach higher-levels of team performance.

Each event in Scrum serves a specific purpose.

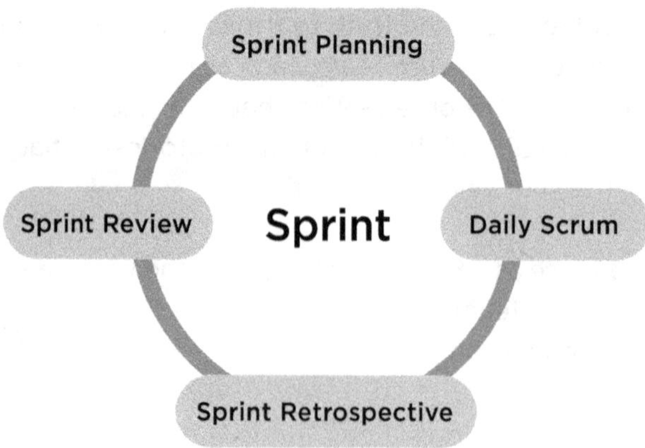

Figure 2.4 The Five Scrum Events

The Sprint

In Scrum, a Sprint is a short, timeboxed period in which a Scrum Team works to complete an Increment of the product. The Sprint acts as a container for the other four events - Sprint Planning, Daily Scrum, Sprint Review and the Sprint Retrospective. In terms of a Sprints duration, these are fixed to one-month or less, with the next Sprint starting immediately after the conclusion of the last Sprint. Only the Product Owner has the authority to cancel a Sprint and the only time this would happen is if the Sprint Goal became obsolete. The Scrum Master acts as a facilitator to help the Scrum Team arrive at a consensus for the Sprint duration.

Sprint Planning

The work to be performed in the Sprint is planned during the Sprint Planning event - this event kick-starts the Sprint. A plan is created by the collaborative efforts of the entire Scrum Team. This event is timeboxed to a maximum of eight hours for a one-month Sprint. For shorter Sprints, the event is normally shorter. Your role as the Scrum Master is to ensure that the event takes place, the participants understand its purpose and for it to be as effective as possible. The Scrum Master coaches the Scrum Team to keep within the timebox. The purpose of the Sprint Planning Event is to create a Sprint Goal and an actionable plan for the Sprint, also known as the Sprint Backlog.

Sprint Planning answers two questions:

- What can be delivered as part of the product Increment in the upcoming Sprint?
- How will the work needed to deliver the product Increment be achieved?

If it's required, the Scrum Team can invite others from outside the team if they wish to assist them to better understand the items of work on the Product Backlog.

Daily Scrum

The Daily Scrum is held by the Developers, for the Developers. It is an essential event for inspection and adaptation. It's an opportunity for the Developers to discuss and agree their plan of action for the next 24-hours on their path towards achieving the Sprint Goal. The Sprint Backlog is updated as necessary, either during the Daily Scrum or following the event. It can be updated as required over the course of the day as more becomes known. It's best to think of it as a 'mini-planning session'. The Daily Scrum is the shortest of the Scrum events and is timeboxed to 15-minutes, that's to say it doesn't need to last the full 15-minutes; if the Developers achieve what they need to in under 5-minutes then that's great! The only time the Product Owner would be required to attend and participate as one of the Developers is if they are also working on Sprint Backlog items during the Sprint. The same applies to the Scrum Master. As the Scrum Master your role is to ensure the event takes place, doesn't exceed the timebox and that it is a productive and positive event for the Developers.

Sprint Review

The purpose of the Sprint Review is for the Developers, the Product Owner, stakeholders and ideally the customer to inspect the outcome of the Sprint and is an opportunity for everyone to review the progress being made towards the Product Goal. How it is run is up to the Scrum Team to decide and there are many ways to do this, but the Scrum Guide™ recommends that it shouldn't be limited to a presentation. This event is timeboxed to a maximum of four hours for a one-month Sprint. For shorter Sprints, the event is normally shorter. Your role as the Scrum Master is to ensure that the Sprint Review takes place, that it is kept to the timebox and that the objectives of the event are reached, e.g. the outcome of the Sprint reviewed, the Product Backlog adjusted accordingly and the progress towards the Product Goal highlighted.

Sprint Retrospective

The Sprint Retrospective is an opportunity for the Scrum Team to pause and reflect on what they did well as a team during the Sprint and what perhaps didn't go as planned, so they can make the next Sprint better. The event is attended by the Developers, the Product Owner, and the Scrum Master. It is timeboxed to a maximum of three hours for a one-month Sprint. For shorter Sprints, the event is normally shorter. To reduce complexity, it is held at the same time and location during each Sprint. Your role as the Scrum Master is to ensure that the event is positive and productive.

To reduce complexity, all of the Scrum events are held at the same time and location during each Sprint.

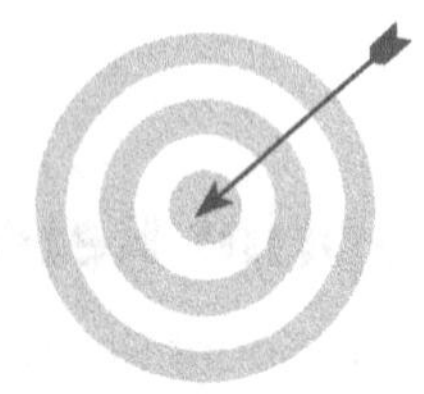

12

Scrum Artefacts

In Scrum, artefacts are 'information radiators' and they serve to capture a shared understanding of the Scrum Team's work and the value being delivered.

There are three Scrum artefacts listed in the Scrum Guide™:

- Product Backlog.
- Sprint Backlog.
- Increment.

Each artefact listed above contains a *commitment* to ensure it provides information that enhances transparency and increases focus against which progress towards to the Sprint Goal can be measured:

- For the Product Backlog the commitment is the Product Goal.
- For the Sprint Backlog the commitment is the Sprint Goal.
- For the Increment the commitment is the Definition of Done.

Product Backlog and Product Goal

The Product Backlog is a prioritised list of all the things that are required by the Scrum Team to produce the product. It is owned by the Product Owner and is the single source of truth for the requirements for the Developers. Product Goals are the big, bold ideas of where the Product Owner imagines their product and their business to be in the future.

Sprint Backlog and Sprint Goal

The Sprint Backlog is a subset of the Product Backlog that the Developers pull into the Sprint to work on. It is essentially the 'to-do list' that the Developers work on during the Sprint. Once the work items from the Product Backlog are added to the Sprint Backlog, these are typically broken-down further into tasks, by the Developers. All items on the Sprint Backlog must meet the Definition of Done to fulfil the commitment. During Sprint Planning, a Sprint Goal is created and added to the Sprint Backlog; it serves as the single objective for the Sprint and acts as the beacon for the Scrum Team to ascertain whether or not they are on track during the Sprint. The Scrum Guide™ stipulates that the Sprint Goal must be finalised prior to the completion of Sprint Planning.

Product Increment and the Definition of Done

The product Increment is the sum of all the work completed within the current and previous Sprints which meet the Definition of Done. The Increment should deliver value to the customer, and shouldn't just be a list of features or tasks added to the product in the latest Sprint. Multiple Increments may be created as part of a single Sprint.

The Definition of Done is a mutual agreement between the Developers and the Product Owner on what constitutes an Increment that is ready for Release. Normally, the Product Owner agrees quality measures with the Developers.

The Definition of Done is created by the Scrum Team. At the point a Product Backlog item meets the Definition of Done, an Increment is born. The Definition of Done should not be confused with Acceptance Criteria, which are the specific conditions an individual Product Backlog item has to fulfil to be accepted by the Product Owner during the Sprint.

The Definition of Done is a very important concept in Scrum and should not be overlooked; neglecting to construct a Definition of Done is a common mistake with new Scrum Teams. The entire point of Scrum is to deliver a 'Done' Increment.

PART 3

Developing People and Teams

It's important to remember that Scrum Teams are like individuals: they take time to grow.

Behavioural team theorists often quote Bruce Tuckman's 'five stages of group development', in that Scrum Teams go through five key phases (forming, storming, norming, performing and adjourning) as they develop and mature.

After a Scrum Team arrives at the performing stage, development truly reaches a new level of awesomeness; members trust each other, understand one another's strengths (and weaknesses), and use that understanding to optimise how they build the product.

Part 3 touches on what's required to build and develop Scrum Teams and ultimately help them succeed in reaching higher levels of performance.

13

Self-Managing Scrum Teams

Self-managing Scrum Teams choose how best to accomplish their work, rather than being directed by others outside the team.

In contrast to traditional management principles, self-managing teams are not directed or controlled from the top; rather they're cross-functional, meaning they have all the skills necessary to create and deliver value, and decide internally between the team members who does what, when, and how.

They typically share decision-making authority, rather than having a centralised decision structure where one person makes all the decisions or even a decentralised decision structure where each team member makes decisions independent of the others.

Self-managing teams offer potential advantages over traditionally managed teams because they bring decision-making authority to the level of operational problems and uncertainties and thus increase the speed and accuracy of problem solving.

Your role as a Scrum Master is to assist teams on their journey to self-management. Through your knowledge and experience you will be able to empower Scrum Teams to achieve their Sprint Goals without any interference or distractions from other areas of the organisation.

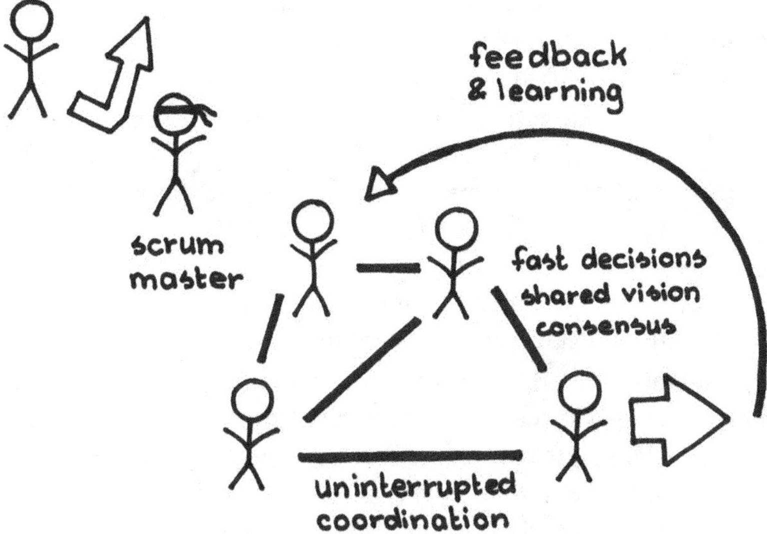

Figure 3.1 Self-Managing Scrum Team

Principles of a Self-Managing Scrum Team

The idea of self-managing Scrum Teams might sound like an easy route to chaos, but when they are developed correctly, that's far from the case. There are several principles that guide self-managing Scrum Teams to help maintain order. These principles include:

- **Collaboration and teamwork:** When a team doesn't have a manager giving orders, it's up to the individual members to communicate with one another and work together to achieve a common goal. As a result, a self-managing team must embrace a highly-collaborative style of working and operate as a cohesive unit.
- **Competency:** Members of a self-managing Scrum Team must exhibit strong confidence in their own capabilities and the capabilities of their team members. This competency is critical since team members cannot expect to receive clear direction from a manager at the start of each project.

- **Regular growth and improvement:** As important as competency is to success, a hunger for regular growth and improvement is equally vital. Without a manager, Scrum Team members must take it upon themselves to seek opportunities for growth and look for ways to improve what they're doing.
- **Trust and respect:** Trust and respect are key ingredients for all Scrum Teams. Team members need to trust in the skills of others and trust that everyone will get the job done as planned, as there is no manager holding everyone accountable. Additionally, team members must respect the opinions of others and work together to find compromises when there are differing views within the team.
- **Motivation:** Working as a self-managing Scrum Team is something of a balancing act. Finding the right skills, establishing high-levels of trust, and ensuring motivation, are keys to success, particularly when there is no manager taking charge. This balancing act makes continuity critical for the team's ongoing success.
- **Ownership:** Finally, self-managing Scrum Team's must exhibit a strong sense of ownership over their process and a commitment to all the principles of self-management set out here in order to propel themselves forward and reach higher-levels of productivity and satisfaction.

Benefits and Challenges of Self-Managing Scrum Teams

Some of the benefits of self-managing Scrum Teams arise from enhanced sharing and learning. This learning can happen from peers and seniors during the frequent interactions and collaboration encouraged by Scrum. Learning also takes place by observing and exposure to cross-functional teams with diverse skills and backgrounds. The frequent interactions also lead to close team bonding and identification with project commitments. Self-managing Scrum Teams encourage active participation by all team members in all Scrum events.

Self-managing teams are important and beneficial for any organisation, but sometimes to build such a team can present a great challenge. They can be difficult to set up, particularly if there is not a culture of using self-managed teams in an organisation. For example, the team may find it difficult to interact with other parts of the organisation because of their different working practices. Individuals new to self-managed teams may be anxious if they perceive that they may be given extra accountabilities. Conversely, team leaders may feel that their role is threatened by having some accountability taken away from them. Everyone may need additional training to give them the extra skills that they may require in their new team.

14

Facilitation

In a Scrum environment, the team depends on the facilitation skills of the Scrum Master to lead the team to higher-levels of performance.

The Scrum Guide™ states that the Scrum Master serves the Product Owner in a variety of ways, including "facilitating stakeholder collaboration as requested or needed". Facilitation is used in a variety of contexts, including training, experiential learning, conflict resolution, and negotiation.

Facilitation is the process of helping groups or individuals learn, find a solution, or reach consensus without imposing or dictating an outcome. Facilitation empowers individuals or groups to learn for themselves or to find their own answers to problems without control or manipulation. To be a good facilitator, Scrum Masters need good communication skills, including listening, questioning, and reflecting.

Facilitation, is also known as the art of hosting, in other words creating an environment and process where people feel sufficiently safe and supported to disclose what they're thinking and feeling. Facilitation provides the framework for your sessions and the context in which your group can move forwards in a different way.

As a Scrum Master, good team facilitation starts with being clear about the content of the meeting or event and answering the question: what it is that you are facilitating?

Think back over any flawed meetings and workshops you've attended in the past. How many meetings failed or were ineffective because it wasn't clear what they were meant to achieve? That's assuming there really was a proper purpose behind them in the first place!

High-performing Scrum Teams are not born overnight. Building synergy takes time and effective facilitation.

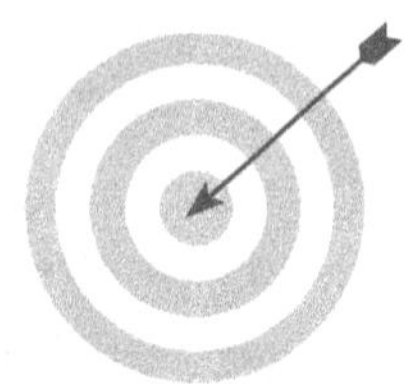

15

Leadership Styles

The Scrum Guide™ states, 'Scrum Masters are true leaders who serve the Scrum Team and the larger organisation'. In other words, a leader who leads and serves at the same time. Scrum Masters should help teams to adopt Scrum and improve their way of working, and serve the team by creating an environment where people can work effectively and are protected from outside interference.

Servant leadership

Servant leaders use listening, empathy, and insight while sharing power and authority with team members. Traditional leadership style is based on power being exercised by one person at the 'top of the pyramid.' So essentially whoever is at the top has the control or the decision-making power.

The Characteristics of being a good servant leader are as follows:

- **Listening:** placing importance on listening to others in the Scrum Team and the organisation, rather than trying to push your own view.
- **Empathy:** understanding others' feelings and points of view.

- **Healing:** encouraging each person's emotional and spiritual health.
- **Awareness:** understanding your own values, feelings, strengths and weaknesses and how these can help or hinder a Scrum Team.
- **Persuasion:** influencing others through your past successes and failures with other Scrum Teams in other organisations.
- **Conceptualisation:** integrating present realities and future possibilities.
- **Foresight:** instinctive feel for how the past, present, and future are connected.

If you use Scrum practices personally, then why not hold a retrospective and think back to how you have used these characteristics recently and how you can improve upon their usage in the future - you can use Scrum practices to improve yourself, too! Only when you become an exceptional servant leader can you truly become a great Scrum Master!

16

Coaching and Mentoring

Coaching

Through coaching, the Scrum Master aims to improve the performance of an individual or team, in pursuit of an objective set by the individual or team. The Scrum Master is accountable for coaching the Developers, the Product Owner, and the Organisation. Coaching empowers and brings out the best in them.

The Scrum Master, in their role as a coach, helps the Scrum Team, as well as the organisation, adopt Scrum and enhance team and enterprise agility.

6 traits of a great coach:

- Find personal satisfaction in seeing others succeed.
- Genuinely care about the people they work with.
- Have a recognisable competence or expertise.
- Possess a great combination of toughness and compassion.
- Are uniquely and authentically themselves.
- Believe in the person they invest in.

Mentoring

This is a relationship in which a more experienced person guides a less experienced person in the performance of their work. It includes the informal transmission of knowledge, as well as psychosocial support to enable broad ongoing development. As the team is engaged in the daily use of Scrum, the Scrum Master helps them use it more effectively. As the Scrum Master, your focus should be on helping the Scrum Team become self-sufficient, and ultimately self-managing.

What's the difference between coaching and mentoring?

Coaching is a set of techniques and practices designed to help the Scrum Team or individual find the answers to their challenges themselves. It carries the underlying premise that those receiving the coaching already know the answer. Mentoring, however, assumes that the Scrum Master knows more than the Scrum Team or individual and is there to impart wisdom, experience, and knowledge in order for the mentee to succeed. In a nutshell, mentoring is concerned with Scrum Team development while coaching is about working with the Scrum Team to improve their performance.

PART 4

Managing Products with Agility

The product must deliver value to customers, so that they actually choose to buy or use it.

Products are rarely perfect on their first release to the customer; frequent iterations incorporating rounds of customer feedback are required to create a product that succeeds and meets real-world customer needs. This means that the product isn't necessarily finished once it gets into the customers hands.

17

Advantages of Managing Products with Agility

One of the advantages of managing products with Agility and incorporating iterative and incremental product delivery is that this makes it possible for organisations to respond immediately to all sorts of changes concerning the product, including:

- Ever-changing customer needs.
- New technologies.
- Evolving opportunities and threats from the business.
- Changes in the marketplace and the industry.

A Scrum Master can assist the Scrum Team and the organisation to manage products with Agility by:

- Coaching the Scrum Team on the need for clear and concise Product Backlog items.
- Understanding product planning in an empirical environment.
- Educating the Product Owner to arrange the items on the Product Backlog in a way that maximises value to the customer.
- Improving their own knowledge on Agility and the different strategies for practicing this.

18

Forecasting

A forecast is a calculated best guess, in other words, a prediction. In Scrum, the Developers are the people in the Scrum Team that are committed to creating any aspect of a usable Increment each Sprint (Scrum Guide™).

During Sprint Planning, the Developers forecast the items they believe will be achieved in the next Sprint. The forecast is made based on what is actually known and what has happened previously and uses empiricism (I covered this in Part 2). The Product Backlog items are added to the Sprint Backlog and this becomes the forecast of work, in that it is not a commitment, or promise, it is an aspiration. The Developers do however make a commitment to achieve the Sprint Goal during the Sprint.

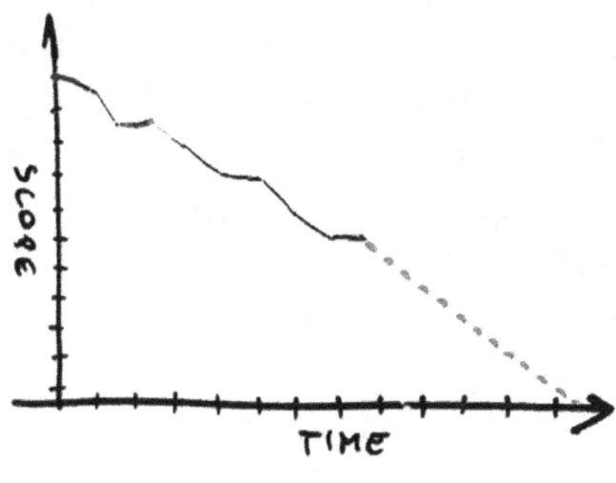

Figure 4.1 Burn-Down Chart

Various practices exist to visualise Sprint progress, like burn-down charts, burn-up charts, or cumulative flow diagrams.

19

Release Planning

Release planning is when various sets of usable functionality or an Increment of the product are planned to be delivered to the customer. Many organisations have their own cadence regarding the release of products to their customers. Some choose to release a product to the customer as part of every Sprint. Others group the results of multiple Sprints into the one release and deliver this to the customer. Still other organisations release the product as soon as each feature meets the Definition of Done, even if this occurs during a Sprint, meaning there could be many releases during a Sprint thus supporting rapid feedback from customers.

The Scrum Guide™ does not make any recommendations or suggestions for how organisations conduct their releases. The decision on how this is done ultimately rests with the organisation.

The release plan is not a static plan which governs the way a Product Owner should manage and order the Product Backlog. When new knowledge is acquired (such as when entries in the Product Backlog are updated and adjusted), the release plan should be revisited and updated accordingly.

A general delivery roadmap of releases establishes trust and manages expectations between the Scrum Team and other stakeholders. Furthermore, release plans should take into account all the additional work that must be accomplished by the Scrum Team, such as training the customer support team, etc.

As a Scrum Master, you can coach the Product Owner to incorporate release planning as part of the Scrum project by assisting them to:

- Define the Product Goal. The Product Owner should consult with stakeholders to ensure their product goal aligns with both the market and the organisation's overall objectives.
- Prioritise the Product Backlog. The Product Owner should outline a basic Scrum release plan or roadmap that includes the release goal, release target date, and the prioritised product requirements.
- Hold a release planning meeting. This step ensures that the Scrum Team and the organisation are on the same page regarding strategy and collaboration before diving into the project.
- Finalise and share the product release calendar. Following the planning meeting, the Product Owner should finalise the details, make any last adjustments, and then share the product release calendar with their stakeholders.

20

Product Value

Scrum is all about value: "Scrum is a lightweight framework that helps people, teams and organizations generate value through adaptive solutions for complex problems." (Scrum Guide™).

As mentioned throughout this book, the Product Owner is responsible for maximising the value of the product.

Product value can be measured in a number of different ways. From my own experience, I have come to realise there is no cookie cutter approach to measuring value; it very much depends on the organisation, product, and the market the product serves.

As a Scrum Master, you can help the measuring of a product's value by coaching the Product Owner to undertake the following activities:

- Involve others. Just as with a Product Goal, stakeholders and the Developers likely have valuable perspectives and ideas. By coaching the Product Owner to involve others, you will help them to feel heard, which is likely to increase their commitment to, and understanding of, the products value.
- Make measures visible. Measures should be transparent to all stakeholders and the Developers. Consider coaching the Product Owner to create a dashboard of value metrics for the product.

- Talk about measures and results in Sprint Reviews. As product features and functionality are being demonstrated to those who attend, encourage the Product Owner to speak about the expected value and what this means for everyone if it is achieved.
- Map everything back to the business goals. Through coaching the Product Owner on relating measures back to the business goals, this creates alignment and helps provide the rationale for how the Product Owner is defining product value. If the business goals change, then that can be a good indicator that the Product Owner needs to inspect and possibly adapt their value definitions and measures.

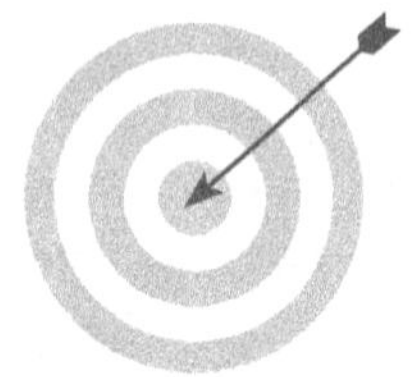

21

Product Backlog Management

To maximise the value delivered to the customer, a Product Owner orders the items in the Product Backlog, with the highest priority items at the top. They can choose to order the Product Backlog in any way they wish. Often, they will consider one or more of the following to help them with this ordering:

- Product value
- Return on investment
- Technical coherence
- Feature coherence
- Technical risk
- Customer adoption
- Cost of delay
- Regulatory/legal compliance

What is considered valuable for a product fluctuates depending upon the nature of the product and the organisation. For some products, the volume of users is a key value measure, while for others it may be product revenue.

Product Owners must decide what value means in their product context. Once agreed, this helps with value-based prioritisation decisions and ordering of the Product Backlog. Product Backlog ordering decisions are assumptions about a future product state. The Product Owner validates these assumptions by gathering data and feedback about the product, ideally from real users.

As a Scrum Master, you can assist the Product Owner by working with them to refine the items on the Product Backlog and ensure that these are clear, concise and ordered, ready for the start of Sprint Planning. You can also work with the Product Owner to ensure that the Product Goal is added to the Product Backlog.

The Product Owner is accountable for effective management of the Product Backlog, but they may also delegate this task to someone else if they need to, whilst still remaining accountable.

PART 5

Developing and Delivering Products Professionally

A high-quality product starts with high-quality requirements; *good requirements drive the quality of the products that are delivered* to the customer.

To deliver high-quality products to customers, the Scrum Master, the Developers and the Product Owner have to jointly ensure the quality of the requirements and manage them effectively. Quality practices have to be ingrained in the Scrum Team's daily work.

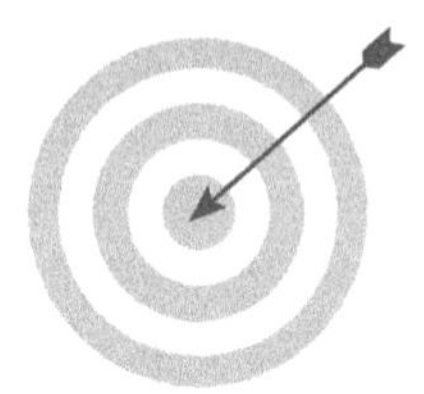

22

Emergent Software Development

Emergent software development refers to the ability to adapt to new ideas, concepts, or discoveries that arise while building a product Increment. To understand what this means, we first need to revisit the Waterfall delivery model; where a product's design is completed and perfected up-front, before its development is even started.

If the customer knows exactly what they want, then a Waterfall approach is the most efficient way to get them the product. However, one of the reasons a large percentage of Waterfall projects fail is because the customer seldom knows exactly what they want.

Emergent software development starts from a completely different perspective, with minimal or no design up front so that the Scrum Team can get to creating the product with the customer as quickly as possible to inform changes to the products design.

The design and build aspect of Scrum happens in parallel, which facilitates tremendous cross-team collaboration and rapid problem-solving. Fires can be put out at the first sign of smoke. Little is left to assumption or intuition.

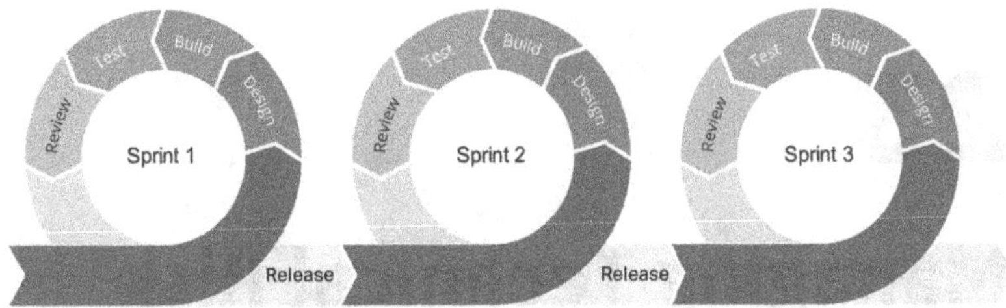

Figure 5.1 Emergent Software Development in Scrum

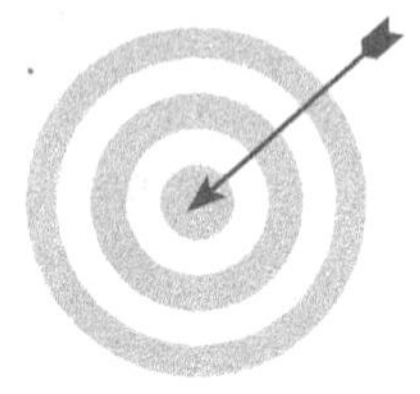

23

Managing Technical Risk

Every Scrum project, irrespective of scale and size, is subject to risk. The information below highlights different ways for how a Scrum Team may choose to handle technical risk.

1 **Flexibility reduces business-environment-related risk**

   Risk is largely minimised in Scrum due to the flexibility of adding or modifying requirements at any time in the project delivery life cycle. This enables the organisation to respond to threats or opportunities from the business environment and unforeseen requirements whenever they arise, with low cost of change as compared to traditional project management methods.

2 **Regular feedback reduces expectations-related risk**

   Being iterative, the Scrum framework gives ample opportunities to obtain feedback and set expectations throughout the project delivery life cycle. This ensures that the project stakeholders, as well as the Scrum Team, are not caught off guard by miscommunicated requirements.

3 **Team ownership reduces estimation risk**

The Scrum Team estimates and takes ownership of the Sprint Backlog items, which leads to more accurate estimation and timely delivery of product Increments.

4 **Transparency reduces non-detection risk**

The Scrum principle of transparency around which the framework is built ensures that risks are detected and communicated early, leading to better risk handling and mitigation. Moreover, when conducting Scrum of Scrum meetings, impediments that one team is facing currently can be recognised as a risk for other Scrum Teams in the future, and that should be recorded in the Updated Impediments Log.

5 **Iterative delivery reduces investment risk**

Continuous delivery of value throughout the Scrum project life cycle, as opposed to the product being delivered at the end of the project as in traditional project management methods, reduces investment risk for the customer.

24

Continuous Quality

Quality should not be something thought about by the Scrum Team towards the end of a project, but rather something that should be built into every step of building the product. This mindset in Scrum Teams has allowed organisations to solidify their pursuit of higher levels of customer satisfaction.

Continuous quality is an integral part of ensuring the Scrum Team delivers a quality product to the customer. The Scrum Team's Definition of Done will drive the level of quality expected by the customer in order for a product to achieve its intended value.

The concept of delivering continuous quality fits readily into the concept of Scrum as it does not require you can only deliver an Increment at the end of a Sprint.

A *Scrum Team* that is focused on continual quality and excellence is more likely to succeed than one that isn't. Quality is the Scrum Team's responsibility.

The Scrum Master helps the Product Owner and the Developers enforce the standards of quality that the Scrum Team has decided upon. Some of the ways a Scrum Master can do this is by:

- making sure that the Scrum Team's processes, methods, and practices are as efficient and effective as possible.

- Ensuring the Scrum Team is cross-functional to reduce external dependencies and the reliance of others outside of the Scrum Team.
- Ensuring the Scrum Team incorporate a Definition of Done that takes into account the quality of a product, so that they know when an Increment is "Done".
- Encourage the Developers to incorporate some quality practices as part of the Sprint Backlog.

PART 6

The Benefits of Acquiring the PSM I

In general, it's easier to secure an interview for a Scrum Master role if you have a Scrum Master certification and it's even easier if your certification is from a recognised institution.

Obtaining the PSM I certification demonstrates your commitment to the profession and your technical knowledge of the Scrum framework.

Perhaps the strongest reason for acquiring your PSM I is to give yourself the best possible chance of securing the career you desire.

The PSM I is recognised worldwide by organisations. As a Scrum Master, having a professional certification in your area of expertise can provide you with a number of benefits.

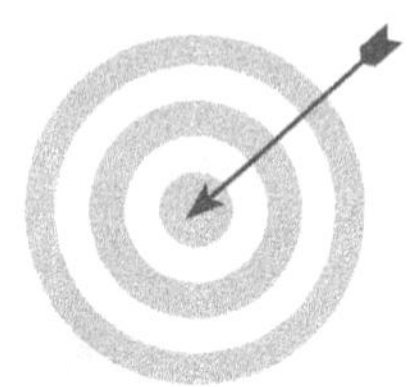

25

Enhanced Professional Credibility

If you are early in your career and want to establish yourself, gaining certification provides a stamp of approval from a reputable organisation.

Anyone can claim to have the leadership, training and coaching skills of a Scrum Master, but certification in this field really adds value to your resume. Certification goes towards demonstrating to your prospected employer or client that you know what you're doing. It provides external validation that you have the skills and knowledge needed to help Scrum Teams succeed.

Certifications create pathways for advancement within an organisation and help establish you as a subject matter expert in your field.

Scrum Master certifications will get you noticed, providing of course that they are the right certifications. Not all certifications are accredited, which means they're not vetted by a well-known education provider or learning institution. Worthwhile certifications will be backed by an accredited institution, and these are the certifications that will be recognised by employers and clients and likely to strengthen your job application. If your Scrum Master certification doesn't come from a recognisable source, then it's likely not to be beneficial to your career.

26

Improved Interaction with Peers

Having a Scrum Master certification will help you to build a better understanding of Scrum while working with your colleagues. It helps to promote productivity while at the same time it can help improve your communication and collaboration with your peers.

This can lead to influencing your organisation to adopting Agile principles and values. Adopting these will help your organisation as it will ensure better yields, less time to market, timely insights, improved productivity, better Return on investment, useful products during each Sprint and much more.

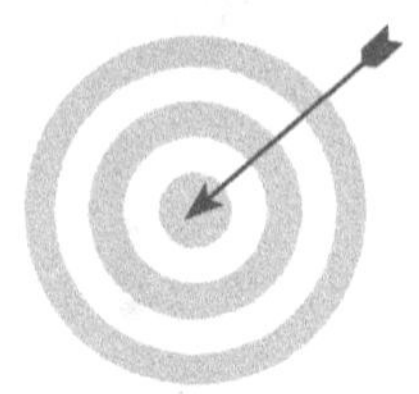

27

Boosted Efficiency, Productivity and Performance

By investing in your professional development, you can achieve greater efficiency, productivity and performance, leading to a more satisfying and fulfilling career as a Scrum Master.

Studies by a variety of organisations — including Microsoft, — have shown that employees with a professional certification are more productive. That's because certifications better prepare individuals to deal with day-to-day challenges and get the most out of new technologies.

Those certified in a particular area of Scrum are able to make greater use of the project or programme's advanced features.

Certified employees often work more efficiently than uncertified colleagues, and their presence can help improve the productivity of Scrum Team projects.

Further Reading

Cushing Anderson, Matthew Marden, Randy Perry (2015): *IT Certifications: Shorter Road to Valuable Positions.*

28

Job Retention

In a volatile economic environment, businesses are always looking for ways to cut costs. That may mean jobs or contracts are on the line. This is when having a professional Scrum Master certification could mean the difference between keeping your job or contract and being forced to seek a new one.

Earning your PSM I demonstrates that you are determined to enhance your skillset and knowledge - which benefits both you and your employer or client. The bottom line is you must invest in yourself.

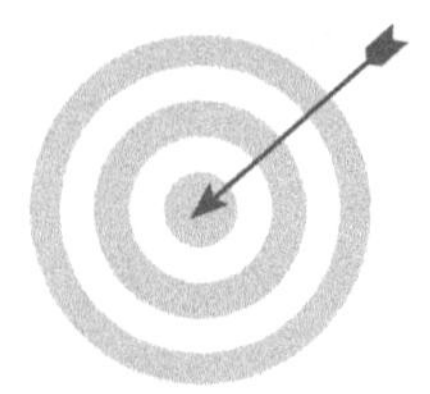

29

Increased Competitive Advantage

The numbers of certified Scrum Masters is on the increase, yet many Scrum Masters still do not see the value in obtaining a professional certification in Scrum. Having a professional certification when your competitors do not sets you apart when you pursue new career opportunities.

Certifications can certainly differentiate you from other professionals in your field, showing that you have a demonstrated commitment to self-development and excelling in your role as a Scrum Master. Having your PSM I could give you the advantage over your competition, which is particularly important in today's highly competitive market.

30

Increased Confidence

The opportunity to feel completely confident in your ability to coach and train any Scrum Team is another crucial factor to take into account when considering whether or not to invest in a professional Scrum Master certification. Quite simply, there is nothing like the feeling of being in control and knowing exactly what you are doing.

On the other hand, if you are currently confused and feel that you are winging it as a Scrum Master then this is bound to have a negative impact on your confidence. By undertaking the PSM I you are validating your knowledge and understanding of the Scrum framework, which will lead to increased confidence in your ability to excel as a Scrum Master.

Speaking from personal experience, when you understand the whole end-to-end process and the best practices used by Scrum Masters around the world, you may start to feel your confidence levels rise. In this way, you can embrace each new challenge, rather being afraid of problems that arise when trying to introduce Scrum to a new organisation.

No matter how big or potentially difficult a new Scrum project appears to be, you will feel ready to take it on and confident in your abilities as a Scrum Master.

31

Global Recognition

The PSM I is recognised globally, making it easier to take on international Scrum Master roles and opportunities.

With businesses becoming increasingly global and converging at a very fast rate, professionals working in virtually any sector need to be prepared to pack up and move in pursuit of new opportunities across the globe.

Maybe it will be a promotion to a more senior role in a regional office of the organisation you work for, or perhaps a new Scrum Master role in an organisation based overseas. Whatever your specific circumstance, having qualifications that are globally recognised is key to gaining an edge over your competition and ensuring you are selected for the job.

Scrum Masters who obtain the PSM I certification are considered highly attractive to international organisations across virtually any industry, from marketing to video game development.

32

Increased Earning Potential

Prospective employers and customers usually consider a person's level of education and their commitment to ongoing professional training and development important when deciding to hire, promote or do business with them. In many companies, a Scrum Master with the required experience may be passed over for a promotion in favour of a candidate with similar experience but more in terms of industry recognised Scrum Master certifications.

Achieving your PSM I means you're serious about contributing to your current or future employers' or clients success by helping them operate more efficiently and profitably. It means you're capable of setting goals and achieving them!

When you obtain the skills employers and clients are seeking, you'll find yourself in demand. It's as simple as that.

The evidence is there. The 2019 Global Scrum Master Trends Report interviewed 2,100 Scrum Masters from across 87 countries and concluded that those who held a Scrum Master certification had a higher salary in comparison to those without.

By investing a relatively small amount of time and effort now, you could be making a huge investment in your future career and earning potential as a Scrum Master.

The only way to do great work is to love what you do.

-STEVE JOBS,
FORMER CEO AND CO-FOUNDER OF APPLE

PART 7

Advice

The best piece of advice I can give you is to learn from others who have walked your path before and successfully passed the PSM I assessment. In the majority of cases, they know what they are talking about from experience.

The advice provided in Part 7 is collectively based on the feedback and suggestions garnered by past PSM I candidates who have shared their experiences via the Scrum.org public forum.

Follow the advice over the next few pages to not only prepare yourself to pass the PSM I assessment, but to achieve the best mark possible!

33

The Scrum Guide™ (2020)

If you only read one thing before taking the PSM I assessment, make sure it is the Scrum Guide™. Then read, eat, sleep and repeat until you are confident that you have fully understood everything, because every sentence in the Scrum Guide™ has a value worth recognising.

The Scrum Guide™ is your definitive guide to Scrum and is considered the *Scrum Body of Knowledge*. It will be your primary source of answers to the PSM I assessment.

The Scrum Guide™ is just 13 pages long, so it's easy to think that a quick thirty-minute read would suffice, but you'd be mistaken. Be sure to study it thoroughly as it covers everything that you'll need to know to pass the PSM I, including the Scrum accountabilities, artefacts, events and the rules that bind these together into a powerful, lightweight framework.

The Scrum Guide™ is available both online and as a printable PDF. You can obtain the latest copy of the Scrum Guide™ direct from the Scrum.org website.

First published in 2010, the Scrum Guide™ has received several updates over the years, with the latest and biggest update being in November 2020, which was to provide further clarity of definitions and the usage of Scrum.

ADVICE

If English isn't your first language, it's worth obtaining a copy of the Scrum Guide™ in your native language. This will reinforce your understanding of Scrum. The Scrum Guide™ is currently available in 30 different languages. Audio books are available, too.

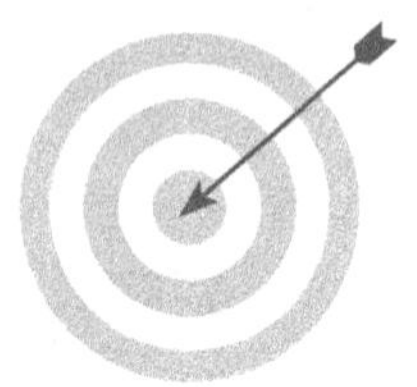

34

Scrum.org Open Assessments

Scrum.org provides a free online Scrum Open Assessment to help prepare you for the PSM family of assessments.

It should be used as a tool for validating your existing knowledge of Scrum and identifying target areas for improvement.

The Scrum Open Assessment is a little kinder than the actual PSM I, allowing you a generous 30 minutes to answer a total of just 30 questions. However, the pass mark still mirrors that of the actual PSM I assessment, with you needing to achieve a minimum score of 85%.

Before taking the Scrum Open Assessment, you should be confident you have fully grasped the information in the Scrum Guide™.

Unfortunately, you do not receive a certificate for successfully passing the Scrum Open Assessment as this is simply a mock exam. A study conducted by Washington University called 'Test-Enhanced Learning' found that students who completed a practice test after a period of revision achieved better results on the final exam compared to students who didn't sit the mock exam and had just spent the whole time revising.

It is strongly recommended by those who have taken the PSM I that you sit the Scrum Open Assessment, as well as the three other Open Assessments available: Product Owner Open, Scrum Developer Open and the Nexus Open, and continue to re-sit these as many times as necessary until you are consistently achieving a pass mark of no less than 100%, for each. The only thing the Open Assessments cost you is time.

You'll be able to access the Scrum Open Assessment directly from the Scrum.org website.

ADVICE

If you fail the Scrum Open Assessment, it's better to have the 'shock in the mock', than the final PSM I exam. The mock exam can act as a call to action that perhaps you need to do more work in a particular area, change your revision strategy or develop the skills needed to perform under pressure. The actual PSM I assessment contains some of the Scrum open Assessment questions, so it's well worth your while attempting these.

35

The Official Glossary of Scrum Terms

Whether you are brand new to Scrum and being a Scrum Master or have coached several cross-functional and self-managing Scrum Teams for years, an in-depth glossary of Scrum terms is still an indispensable tool.

Before even attempting the PSM I exam, you should be familiar with the terminology used in Scrum. The official Glossary of Scrum Terms represents an overview of the terminology used in Scrum and should be your main resource for ensuring you have the right understanding of the terminology used.

Reviewing and understanding each of the terms used in the official Scrum glossary will dramatically increase your chances of successfully passing the PSM I exam. It will also make it easier for you to absorb and understand the information contained in the Scrum Guide™.

Part 10 of this book provides a detailed breakdown of the terminology used in Scrum.

The Glossary of Scrum Terms is not to be confused with other Agile glossaries; these tend to encompass terminology taken from other Agile frameworks rather than being specifically about Scrum.

ADVICE

You may need to unlearn some of the bad habits that you might have picked up over time, such as labelling the Daily Scrum the Daily Stand-Up. The Daily Stand-Up is not part of the Scrum framework and is part of Extreme Programming (XP), which is a separate Agile framework to Scrum.

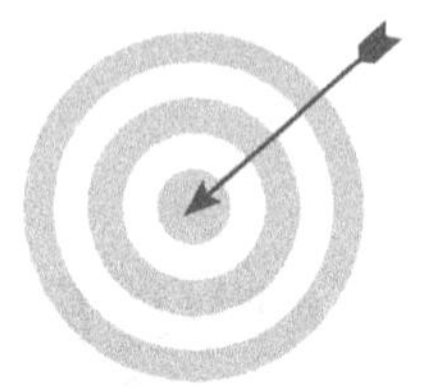

36

The Scrum Forum

The Scrum Forum is an online community where groups of people connect over shared experiences and have discussions about Scrum and PSM I-related topics.

You'll need to register and create a free account to use the forum and agree to Scrum.org's terms of use. Once logged in, you can ask questions, put forward suggestions and share your knowledge, experience and ideas with other like-minded professionals.

Those who have walked your path before you and have previous experiencing of undertaking the PSM I assessment are more than happy and willing to answer any questions that you may have.

To access the Scrum forum, visit the Scrum.org website and search for the 'Community' page.

If you're new to forums in general, it's a good idea to read posts on the Scrum forum for a little while before you create a new post. If you want people to respond to your posts, you need to become an active participant in Scrum forum discussions. Don't just post queries; give answers to questions, too, and do so as frequently as you have something valuable to add. You don't have to be an all-knowing expert to answer a question; you can always describe your experience with the topic at hand rather than giving hard-and-fast advice.

ADVICE

People don't like answering the same question multiple times. If you have a general question, search the forum for that question before you create a post. Your question may have already been answered thoroughly in a previous conversation. Granted this may take you some additional time, but it may also help you to get to your answer quicker rather than waiting for a response from another member of the forum.

37

Third-Party Practice Tests

Once you begin to research sample PSM I questions and answers online, you'll undoubtedly stumble upon various third-party organisations offering either free or paid-for practice assessments that promise to help prepare you for the PSM I exam.

Whist taking a test offered by a third-party may seem like a good idea, there are a few things to consider. Firstly, the practice tests offered have not been endorsed by Scrum.org. There are lots of reasons for this but the main one is that many of these third-party providers do not use the official materials produced by Scrum.org, so there is a risk that they could be misleading and you may learn incorrect information and terminology, leading you to a state of confusion.

Whilst the tests may be able to give you a rough indication of where you stand in terms of your knowledge and understanding of Scrum, they may also damage your chances of passing the assessment by giving you an inaccurate picture.

It is unlikely that a third-party will be able to replicate the style and nuances of the actual PSM I exam for legal reasons. Some third-party providers (but not all) are likely to overemphasise some concepts, whilst omitting others entirely. Questions may also be too easy or too hard, again, not offering you a true reflection of the actual assessment. However, most reputable third-party organisations will state that their assessments whilst similar, are not the same as the questions in the actual PSM I exam.

Whilst there is a practice assessment included as part of this book, again, this has not been endorsed by Scrum.org and is not an exact replication of the PSM I assessment for legal reasons.

ADVICE

If you do decide to sit practice tests offered by third-parties and then later decide to enrol onto a 2-day PSM I training course offered by a Scrum.org certified Professional Scrum Trainer, you may have difficulty unlearning some of the misinformation you have acquired as part of the third-party practice tests that you undertook, so it's worth doing some background research on the third-party and their affiliation with Scrum.org before making a financial commitment.

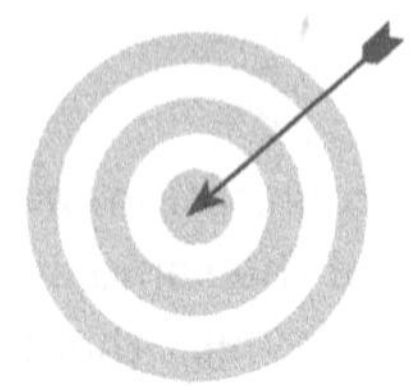

38

PSM I Training

If self-study alone proves to be too challenging, you could always opt for some Professional Scrum Master training from Scrum.org.

A PSM I training course is a two-day course that covers the principles and the empirical process theory underpinning the Scrum framework and the role of the Scrum Master in it. The course is a combination of instruction and team-based exercises, and teaches what is at the heart of the Scrum framework. You'll learn how to use Scrum to optimise value, productivity and the total cost of product ownership.

Each Scrum.org certified Professional Scrum Trainer (PST) will generally put their own spin on the course; however, all PST's are required to use the same base-line training materials so that candidates are learning the same content across the board, regardless of where in the world the training is being conducted and which PST is running the training course.

Scrum.org believes consistency is key; everyone who attends their training courses is learning the same message and, ultimately, the single most authentic source of truth taken directly from the Scrum Guide™.

If you do decide to attend the formal training offered by Scrum.org, the PSM I exam fee will be included as part of your training cost, and you will be emailed an online voucher following the end of day two, giving you a single attempt at taking the assessment.

Whilst it's certainly not mandatory, preparing for the PSM I assessment without some form of expert assistance is probably a bad idea, but this does depend on your individual experience with Scrum; many Scrum Masters have successfully sat the exam without any form of expert assistance.

ADVICE

Attending a course on Scrum is not a mandatory requirement to take the PSM I assessment. If you feel that you already possess a high-level of Scrum knowledge, understanding of the Scrum Guide™ and how to apply Scrum within Scrum Teams, Scrum.org invites you to take the PSM I assessment directly. However, there is a PSM I course available to help you prepare for the assessment and gain a stronger understanding of Scrum if you feel this is necessary.

39

Open Book Assessment

The PSM I assessment is an open-book assessment, which means you have the option to take notes, text or resource materials into your self-proctored assessment.

The open-book nature of the PSM I assessment may make it sound easy to pass, but don't let that fool you into thinking that you'll be able to take a copy of the Scrum Guide™ into the assessment and breeze your way through to the 85% pass mark, because it's not that simple!

Forty-five seconds is only just enough time to read the question, make sure you understand what it's asking, look through the possible answers and then select an answer. Now imagine doing all of the above and having to sift your way through the Scrum Guide™ in addition. It would become almost impossible due to the limited amount of time available to you.

Taking materials into the assessment may only serve as a distraction. Once you've read and understood the Scrum Guide™, you simply won't need anything else to assist you.

The assessment has purposely been constructed in this way to ensure that those who do pass do so because they actually know the answer and are therefore worthy of holding the PSM I certification.

ADVICE

If you do decide to take materials into the exam, be sure to carefully select these and organise them in a way that allows you to reference what you need, quickly. You wouldn't be the first person to do this and I'm sure that you wouldn't be the last. The choice sits entirely with you as only you know if you'd be capable of referencing materials during the assessment without these becoming a distraction.

40

The Nexus Framework

Nexus is a framework consisting of roles, events, artefacts, and techniques that bind and weave together the work of approximately three to nine Scrum Teams working from a single Product Backlog to build an integrated Increment that meets a common goal.

The Nexus framework was created by Ken Schwaber in 2015 and is largely based on the Scrum framework, using Scrum as its basic building blocks.

Nexus is a process framework for multiple Scrum Teams working together to create an integrated Increment. Nexus is consistent with Scrum and its parts will be familiar to those who have used Scrum. The difference is that more attention is paid to dependencies and interoperation between Scrum Teams, delivering at least one 'Done' *integrated Increment* every Sprint.

Getting familiar with the Nexus framework may prove to be beneficial for the PSM I assessment. Although the PSM I assessment does not specifically include any Nexus-related questions, you may still encounter questions concerning multiple Scrum Teams and, therefore, scaled Scrum.

Nexus essentially extends Scrum to guide multiple Scrum Teams on how they work together to deliver working software in every Sprint.

ADVICE

It is important to remember that even scaled Scrum is still just Scrum, so it's imperative to keep the core fundamentals and values underpinning Scrum in mind when answering any questions about multiple Scrum Teams.

41

Professional Scrum Trainer (PST)

If you're already looking to the future and are considering a career as a certified Professional Scrum Trainer with Scrum.org, then you'll actually need to achieve a minimum pass mark of 95% on the PSM I assessment. This may sound challenging but in reality it only equates to an answering an addition eight questions correctly.

There are eight different steps to becoming a PST, and a pass mark of at least 95% on the PSM I assessment is just one of them.

95% doesn't leave much margin for error. With 80 questions on the PSM I exam, this would mean that you would need to answer 76 questions correctly, out of 80.

Don't worry if you don't achieve 95% on your first or even second attempt, there isn't a set limit on the number of times you can retake the PSM I. Some people have even been known to purchase the assessment and look through the questions without really attempting to pass, just to get a feel for the level expected by Scrum.org.

Obtaining a score of 95% is certainly possible and lots of PSM I holders claim to have achieved in excess of 95% on their first attempt.

ADVICE

Have a look through the discussions on the Scrum forum as there are people on there who've achieved 95% or above on the PSM I and have lots of useful tips and advice to share with you for achieving a high score.

42

Google Translate

Whilst the Scrum Guide™ is available in thirty different languages, the PSM I assessment is available in just the one: English. Additional time is not awarded to those who do not speak English as their first language.

Quite often people observe that one word in the English language can have at least two different meanings in their native language, making the already challenging PSM I assessment even harder to pass.

With just 45 seconds to read and answer a question in the PSM I exam correctly, there isn't time to browse online dictionaries and try to look up the meaning of words.

However, there is some good news. Google's free multilingual machine translation service, 'Google Translate', instantly translates the words, phrases and web-pages between English to over 100 other languages.

ADVICE

Just be aware that it's easier for Google Translate to convert German to English (for example), as the two languages share so much, but other languages such as Chinese to English are not as straightforward due to their complexities and differences.

PART 8

Tips & Tricks

The PSM I assessment doesn't just test your knowledge of Scrum; it also tests your ability to read information and correctly interpret the question being asked whilst under pressure.

To do well in the exam, you need to lay the best possible foundations for success. Follow these six proven tips and tricks to maximise your chances of being awarded the PSM I certification.

43

Attend vs. Participate

Trick 1

Some PSM I questions are purposely written in a way that ensures you genuinely understand the question being asked and that you're not winging it (so to speak).

Below is an example of an 'attend' versus 'participate' type question.

> **Who can attend the Daily Scrum?**
>
> **A.** Anyone
>
> **B.** Only the Developers
>
> **C.** Only the Developers and the Product Owner
>
> **D.** Only the Developers and the Scrum Master

The trick here lies in your ability to distinguish between the word *attend*, which has a different meaning to the word *participate*. The former implies a passive attendance (e.g. to simply observe), whereas the latter denotes an active participation in the Daily Scrum. Only the Developers are required to participate in the Daily Scrum, whereas *anyone can attend* providing they do not interrupt or distract the Developers.

The correct answer is 'A - Anyone'.

TIP

60 minutes is not long, so you need to get used to thinking quickly. You need to be comfortable and capable of reading each question at least twice during the assessment to ensure you understand the true nature of the question being asked.

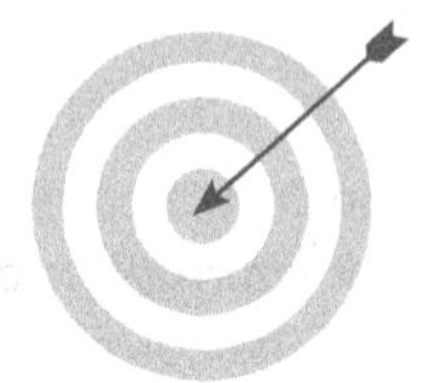

44

Should vs. Could

Trick 2

One of the hardest type of questions you'll come across during the assessment is a 'should' versus 'could' type question. Remember, it's not a case of Scrum.org looking to catch you out or trick you as such, but more that there are so many misconceptions about Scrum that the exam setters want to make sure you know and understand the differences between what's true and what's false.

Below is an example of a 'should' versus 'could' type question.

The Product Owner could attend the Daily Scrum

A. True

B. False

It is true that the Product Owner *could* attend the Daily Scrum, although they don't need to attend. However, under pressure, you might misinterpret could for should and select the incorrect answer. It's easily done.

The correct answer is 'A - True'.

TIP

With a minimum pass mark of 85%, you'll need to pay careful attention to the questions being asked in the assessment. Keep calm and read each question carefully. Feeling under pressure can lead to avoidable mistakes. You've got this!

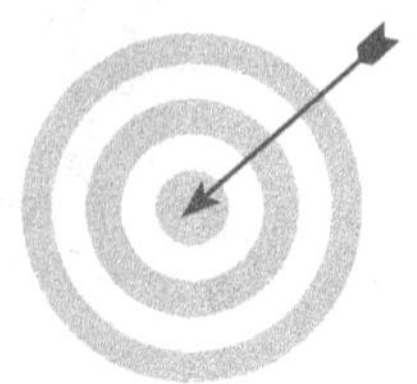

45

Multiple Answers

Trick 3

You may encounter a PSM I question that requires you to select more than one answer, but under pressure, this can be easily overlooked. If you only select one answer where two answers are required, the assessment still allows you to progress onto the next question and doesn't alert you to the fact that you've missed an additional answer.

The PSM I assessment doesn't award marks for partially correct answers, so in the event that this happens, you are awarded zero marks in total for that question.

Below is an example of a multiple answer question.

What are the two primary ways a Scrum Master keeps the Developers working at their highest-level of productivity?

A. By keeping high value features high in the Product Backlog

B. By removing impediments that hinder the Developers

C. By facilitating Developer discussions with stakeholders

D. By starting and ending the events at the proper time

It is the Product Owners responsibility to firstly determine what constitutes value and secondly, ensure that the highest value features remain at the top of the Product Backlog. A Scrum Master can assist the team with keeping events within their timebox, however this wouldn't be considered a primary way for helping to Developers to reach peak levels of productivity.

The correct answers are 'B' and 'C'.

TIP

If you find yourself struggling to decipher between two correct answers, look at the question again to see if it's in fact asking for two answers and not just the one; this could be an indication that the question is looking for two correct answers. Try to spend some time at the end of the assessment going back through the questions and double-checking to see if you've missed any questions where multiple answers are required.

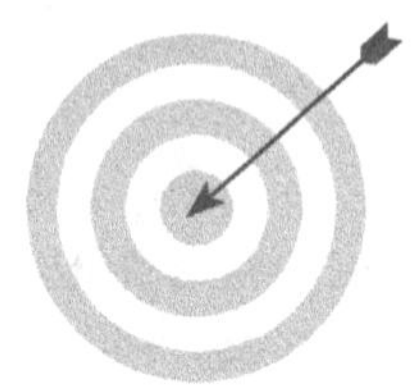

46

'Not' Questions

Trick 4

Be careful when reading a question during the assessment that contains the word 'not'. These are commonly asked throughout the PSM I assessment and less so in the practice tests offered by Scrum.org, making it an unwelcome surprise when you first come across these during the actual assessment.

Below is an example of a 'not' question.

Which of the following is not a Scrum Value:

A. Courage

B. Focus

C. Openness

D. Earned Value

The five Scrum Values are - Commitment, Courage, Focus, Respect and Openness.

The correct answer is 'D - Earned Value'.

TIP

Once you understand the question being asked, write down your task. For example, if a question asks, 'Which of the following is NOT a Scrum Value?' your task might be able to 'eliminate choices that are a Scrum Value.' This will give you a clear idea as to how to approach the answer choices.

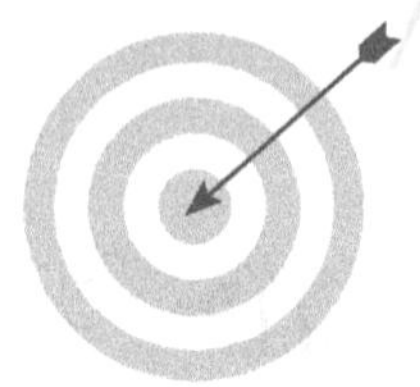

47

Scrum.org vs. Scrum Alliance

Trick 5

Whilst some would argue that there aren't any differences between the PSM I and the CSM (Certified Scrum Master - a similar assessment offered by the Scrum Alliance), the reality is, there are a few slight differences and Scrum.org would like you to be aware of these differences.

If you have previously attended a CSM course, you will need to be aware of what these variances are so that you can avoid falling into the trap of answering a PSM I question with your CSM hat on.

Below is an example of a 'Scrum.org' versus 'Scrum Alliance' question.

What is the recommended size for a Scrum Team?

A. 3-9

B. 7 plus or minus 2

C. 10 or fewer people

D. 9

Scrum.org recommends a Scrum Team size of 10 or fewer people, whereas the Scrum Alliance recommends a team size of 7 plus or minus 2. The difference is subtle, but just enough to cost you a mark.

The correct answer is 'C – 10 or fewer people'.

TIP

Whether you've attended a CSM with the Scrum Alliance or played the role of a Scrum Master during your career, you will likely need to unlearn some of the misinformation you have accumulated. When preparing for the assessment you may need to treat it as if you are reading the Scrum Guide™ and learning about Scrum for the first time.

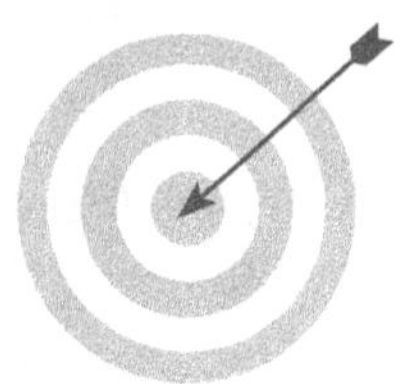

48

Rules and Recommendations

Trick 6

Recommendations are meant to provide guidance whereas rules are meant to be applied strictly, and without exception. Below is an example of a 'rules' versus 'recommendation' question.

The Scrum Team must be no larger than 10 members:

A. True

B. False

Scrum.org only recommends that Scrum Team sizes have 10 or fewer people, but this isn't something that they strictly enforce. This isn't considered to be a 'rule' in Scrum.

The correct answer is 'B - False'.

If you compare the original Scrum Guide™, written in 2010, with the newer version written in 2020, you will notice that Scrum overall is moving away from strict prescriptions. For example, there is no longer a suggestion made as to how the Developers approach the Daily Scrum, whereas in previous iterations it was suggested that the Developers use the following three questions:

1. What did I do yesterday that helped the Scrum Team meet the Sprint Goal?
2. What will I do today to help the Scrum Team meet the Sprint Goal?
3. Do I see any impediment that prevents me or the Scrum Team from meeting the Sprint Goal?

TIP

The latest Scrum Guide™ does prescribe a few rules, such as no changes are made during the Sprint that would endanger the Sprint Goal being met. An easy way to understand what is a recommendation and what is a rule is to take a highlighter pen and go through the Scrum Guide™ highlighting everything that Scrum prescribes. Areas of the guide which aren't highlighted can then be taken as a recommendation.

PART 9

Comparison Between PSM I & CSM

Over the past few years, the job market has witnessed an exponential growth in the demand for Scrum Masters. With varying certifications to choose from, it can be confusing to know which route to take.

There are, however, two Scrum Master certifications that stand out from the rest and it's no coincidence that they are the most popular, too: the PSM I and the Certified Scrum Master (CSM) certification offered by the Scrum Alliance. The PSM I and the CSM are positioned similarly to each other in that they are both entry-level certifications.

There are many factors to consider when deciding between the various Scrum Master certifications and the different institutions that offer them. This part of the book explores the key differences between these two market-leading Scrum Master certifications.

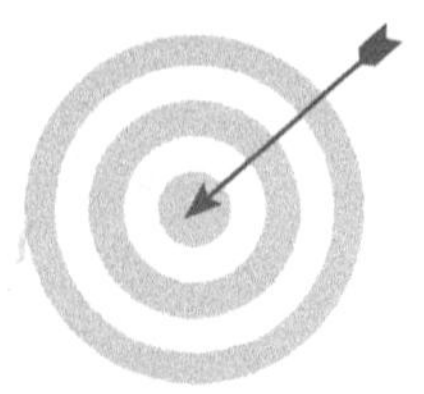

49

History of Scrum Alliance and Scrum.org

Following the creation of the Agile Manifesto in 2001, Ken Schwaber, Mike Cohn and Esther Derby founded the Scrum Alliance in 2002.

The Scrum Alliance was the first organisation to offer a certification for aspiring Scrum Masters - the Certified Scrum Master (CSM).

In 2009, one of the founders, Ken Schwaber, resigned from the organisation and subsequently founded Scrum.org and created a competing entry-level Scrum Master certification - the Professional Scrum Master - Level 1 (PSM I).

Ken left the Scrum Alliance due to disagreeing with the premise that candidates could attend a two-day training course and be awarded a Scrum Master certification - without having to sit an exam to test their level of knowledge and understanding. Upon completing the training course, candidates were then branding themselves as certified Scrum experts. Ken made it his mission to offer a certification that was tougher, so that it guaranteed that candidates who passed possessed a superior understanding of Scrum and how to best apply it within an organisation.

The Scrum Alliance remains the largest certification and membership organisation for Agile and Scrum. At the time of publication, approximately 750,000 people worldwide have obtained a Scrum certification from the Scrum Alliance, compared with 279,000 from Scrum.org.

For up-to-date figures, please visit the Scrum Alliance and Scrum.org websites directly.

You may be wondering why a book about the PSM I has a section dedicated to the CSM. I too wondered the same and after removing it from the book several times, decided to leave it in simply because I want to make sure you are making the right decision based on all the information available to you. If anything, the information pertaining to the next few pages may further solidify your decision to take the PSM I over the CSM.

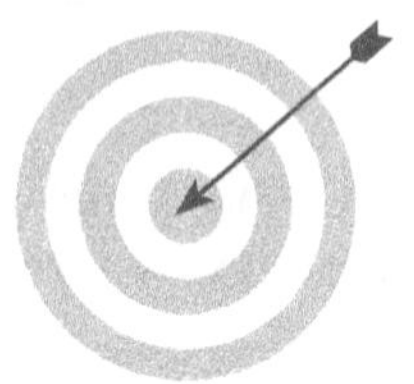

50

The PSM I and CSM

We've covered this already, but just in case you overlooked this the Professional Scrum Master - Level 1 (PSM I) is an entry-level Scrum Master certification offered by Scrum.org.

The Certified Scrum Master (CSM) is an entry-level Scrum Master certification offered by the Scrum Alliance.

51

Exam Prerequisites

The PSM I doesn't have any prerequisites to take the exam. Whilst Scrum.org do have PSM I training courses available, they state that attending a course is not required if you feel you already possess a high-level of Scrum knowledge; if you have a good understanding of the Scrum Guide™ and applying Scrum within Scrum Teams, you are welcome to sit the exam.

In contrast, two solid days of Scrum Master training are required to take the CSM exam, although there are no prerequisites to attend the training.

The PSM I training is conducted by a Scrum.org Professional Scrum Trainer (PST) and the CSM training is conducted by a Scrum Alliance Certified Scrum Trainer (CST).

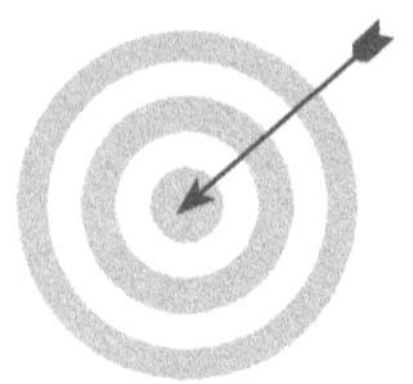

52

The Cost

The minimum cost of obtaining the PSM I is the cost of the exam itself, currently $150 US Dollars. As mentioned, attending a training course is considered optional and incurs an additional cost.

The CSM, however, requires you to attend a two-day training course. Currently courses cost in the region of $500 to $2,500 US Dollars, depending on the trainer. The exam fee is generally included and allows for two attempts at the exam, after this you are liable for the exam costs.

53

Certification Renewal

The CSM is only valid for a period of two years, after which you pay a renewal fee of $100 US Dollars, which is the equivalent to $50 US Dollars per year. In addition, the Scrum Alliance also requires you to earn a certain number of SEU's (Scrum Education Units) to demonstrate that you have been active in the world of Scrum over the last two years. An SEU is a credit earned by completing an educational training or learning opportunity that furthers your knowledge as a Scrum practitioner.

The PSM I is a lifetime certification, meaning that it does not require any form of renewal. Once you've achieved your PSM I, that's it. Mission accomplished.

54

Certification Format

The exam formats are also different. The PSM I consists of multiple-choice questions, multiple answer questions and true or false questions.

The CSM is made up of multiple-choice questions only.

55

Exam Duration

Both Scrum.org and the Scrum Alliance allow you an hour to take the exam. You are not able to pause either exam during the one-hour timebox. Previously, the CSM did allow for you to pause the exam and return to it when you wanted, but this feature has since been removed.

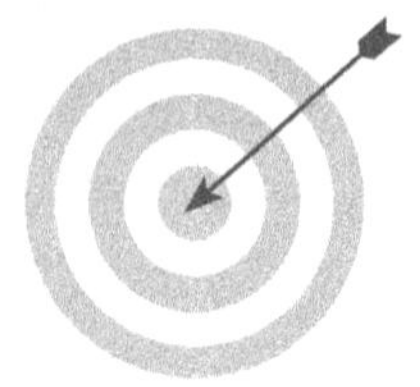

56

Number of Questions

The PSM I has a total of 80 questions. Answering 80 questions inside the 60-minute timebox gives you a maximum of just 45 seconds to read and answer each question correctly.

The CSM has a total of 50 questions, allowing for 72 seconds for each question.

57

Minimum Pass Mark

The pass mark for the PSM I is 85% (68 correct answers out of a total of 80 questions), whereas the pass mark for the CSM is lower in comparison at 74% (37 correct answers out of a total of 50 questions).

Prior to 2020, the CSM use to consist of 35 questions, with a pass mark of just 69% (24 correct answers out of 35). During 2019, the number of questions and the pass mark percentage were increased to increase the level of difficulty.

58

Difficulty Rating

The PSM I is a harder exam in comparison to the CSM simply because you have 30 more questions to answer in the same amount of time, giving you less time to spend on each question.

The pass mark for the PSM I is also higher than that of the CSM.

Because the PSM I is perceived to be the more challenging out of the two qualifications due to its rigorous exam, some organisations believe it to be more credible.

It is doubtful that someone without any prior knowledge and experience of implementing Scrum could pass the PSM I, whereas there have been cases of people who are completely new to Scrum passing the CSM exam after attending a weekend training course.

Whilst the Scrum Alliance's certification numbers are impressive, you could argue that more people hold certifications with the Scrum Alliance over Scrum.org because fewer people are able to pass the PSM I exam. Or to put it another way, the CSM exam is easier to pass, so more people have passed it.

59

Exam Window

Once you've paid the exam fee to take the PSM I, you are free to sit the exam whenever you feel ready, be it in a week's time or a year. The assessment passwords do not expire and remain valid until they are used.

If you decide to pursue the CSM exam, you must complete it within 90 days of attending your CSM training course. It is best to sit an exam as soon as possible following any form of training as the information is still fresh in your memory.

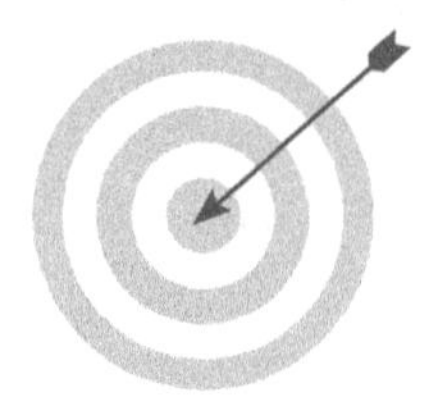

60

Not Passing the Exam

If you fail the PSM I, you will need to purchase the exam again at your own expense. However, if you are taking the exam through a PST, you should check with them directly to see if they offer a free second attempt at the exam.

If, for whatever reason, you do not pass the CSM on your first attempt, you can attempt the exam again for free. However, the Scrum Alliance currently charge $25 US Dollars per attempt for third and subsequent attempts.

Table 9.1 PSM and CSM Comparison Table

Certification Criteria	PSM I (Scrum.org)	CSM (Scrum Alliance)
Number of Questions	x 80	x 50
Pass Mark Questions	68 questions answered correctly	37 questions answered correctly
Pass Mark Percentage	85%	74%
Exam Duration	60 minutes	60 minutes
Required Course Attendance	Optional	Mandatory
Perceived Difficulty Level	Intermediate	Beginner

Certification Criteria	PSM I (Scrum.org)	CSM (Scrum Alliance)
Certification Expiry	Lifetime Validity	Every 2 Years
Fee	*$150 US Dollars	*$500+ US Dollars (Includes training course)
Language	English	English
Exam Format	Multiple Choice, Multiple Answer and True/ False	Multiple Choice

**Please check with Scrum.org and the Scrum Alliance for the latest information on pricing.*

PART 10

The Scrum Glossary

The terminology used in Scrum can be confusing. As an experienced Scrum Master you've likely introduced either your current organisation or a previous organisation to Scrum and the terminology associated with it. You've also likely come across individuals within those organisations who have perhaps misinterpreted terminology used in Scrum. As a Scrum Master, you are accountable for correcting people if they use Scrum terminology incorrectly.

Part 10 is designed to refresh your knowledge of the terminology and ensure that you are using it consistently across the Scrum Teams that you coach.

61

Scrum Terminology

Your Guide to Passing the PSM I Assessment would not be complete without ensuring you have an iron-clad grasp of the Scrum terms that you'll likely encounter during the assessment. This section of the Scrum overview will present the common terminology used in Scrum.

The Scrum Glossary has largely been taken from the official *Glossary of Scrum Terms* from Scrum.org, which is available in over 20 languages (including Arabic, Greek, Persian and Ukrainian). The Scrum Glossary is also aligned with the latest 2020 version of the Scrum Guide™.

This comprehensive glossary is in alphabetical order and provides an overview of Scrum-related terms.

A glossary is often overlooked in books preparing you for the assessment but it is a vital tool; this glossary goes a bit deeper into the terminology commonly seen in relation to Scrum. Reviewing the glossary is a quick and easy way to learn and understand the key terms used throughout the Scrum Guide™.

As an experienced Scrum Master, you should already be familiar with a number of these terms, but in the PSM I exam you don't get marks for being familiar with the subject; you get marks for recalling relevant information and using it to answer the question. A powerful feeling of familiarity is not a guarantee that you can recall the terms correctly.

To understand how these Scrum terms are connected to each other, it is highly recommended that you reference the latest copy of the Scrum Guide™ for a more complete understanding.

62

Terminology from the Scrum Guide™

Burn-Down Chart

A graphical representation of the work remaining on the Sprint Backlog (see Sprint Backlog) that has yet to reach the Definition of Done (see Definition of Done). The burn-down chart can be used to predict the team's likelihood of completing the work in the time-frame available. A burn-down chart is usually an x-y grid. The work remaining is usually depicted on the vertical axis, with time along the horizontal axis. Please refer to Figure 4.1

Burn-Up Chart

A graphical representation of the work completed on the Sprint Backlog that has reached the Definition of Done. The burn-up chart can be used to predict the

Scrum Team's (see Scrum Team) likelihood of completing the work in the time-frame available. A burn-up chart is usually an x-y grid. The work completed is usually depicted on the vertical axis, with time along the horizontal axis.

C

Coherent/ Coherence

Having a Sprint Goal (see Sprint Goal) in Scrum is crucial. What's important to remember is the Sprint Goal can be any other form of coherence providing it helps the Scrum Team to move forward in the same direction during the Sprint (see Sprint), and collaboratively, rather than working on separate initiatives.

D

Daily Scrum

This is typically a 15-minute event that takes place at the same time and place each day. It's specifically for the Developers (see Developers) so they can synchronise their activities and plan their work for the coming day. It's an opportunity for the Scrum Team to inspect its progress towards the Sprint Goal and adjust as needed.

Definition of Done

A shared understanding across the Scrum Team that drives the quality of work and is used to assess whether the work has been completed. Having a Definition of Done removes ambiguity. The moment a Product Backlog (see Product Backlog) item meets the Definition of Done, an Increment (see Increment) is born.

Developer

Accountable for delivering a potentially releasable Increment of Done product during the Sprint. The Developers skills are broad and should contain all of the expertise necessary to deliver the product Increments.

Emergence

At the beginning it's difficult to know everything that there is to know about a product. As more is learned though iterative and incremental delivery, we learn more about what is possible. In Scrum (see Scrum), this is referred to as emergence.

Empiricism

Scrum is based on the empirical process, or empiricism, where decisions are made based on fact and what is known through observation and experience rather than assumptions. The Scrum framework is upheld by the three pillars of empiricism: transparency, inspection and adaptation .

Forecast (or functionality)

When a Scrum Team commits to a selection of items from the Product Backlog based on what it believes is achievable for a given Sprint, this is known as a forecast of the functionality it believes it can deliver.

I

Increment

The sum of the Product Backlog items completed during a Sprint. The Increment must be in a usable condition so that it provides value and meets the Scrum Team's Definition of Done. The sum of the Increments forms the Product.

P

Product Backlog

The process of breaking down items on the Product Backlog so that these are smaller and more understood by the Scrum Team. Additional information is added as necessary such as product details and size. The items are then ordered (with the highest-value items at the top) as necessary by the Product Owner. The process of refinement is undertaken as often as required by the Product Owner.

Product Backlog Refinement

The process of keeping the Product Backlog updated (see Product Backlog). Items are ordered (with the highest-value items at the top) and additional information is added as necessary. Product Backlog Refinement is an ongoing process and is undertaken as often as is required by the Product Owner.

Product Goal

The Product Goal encapsulates the Product Owners vision for the completed product. Similar to an objective, it can provide the Scrum Team with direction for them to plan against. It remains as part of the Product Backlog with the Product Backlog items all being created to eventually deliver the Product Goal. It could be a service, physical product or something else altogether.

Product Owner

The person on the Scrum Team accountable for maximising the value of the Product created by the Developers. The Product Owner is one person and represents the needs of the business, stakeholders (see Stakeholder) and customers. The Product Owner is also known in Scrum as the *value maximiser*. They are also responsible for defining and communicating the Product Goal (see Product Goal).

Ready

Requirements on the Product Backlog that meet a certain set of criteria, giving an indication to the Scrum Team that they are in a place whereby they can be pulled into a Sprint and worked on are known as "Ready".

Scrum

An Agile framework for developing, delivering and sustaining complex products. The framework is an iterative and incremental approach to development and begins with a simple premise: start with what is known. The name comes from rugby, where Scrum is a team formation and everyone plays a specific role and works towards a common goal.

Scrum Guide™

The Scrum Guide™ is a free definitive guide to Scrum for current and aspiring Scrum professionals. Written by the co-founders of Scrum, Ken Schwaber and Jeff Sutherland, it contains the definition of Scrum, including the Scrum Team accountabilities, Scrum events and Scrum artefacts. This is a tool that the Scrum Master should reference on a regular basis.

Scrum Master

Accountable for establishing Scrum within an organisation as per the Scrum Guide™, ensuring its correct application. The Scrum Master is accountable for the Scrum Team's effectiveness. They coach the Scrum Team on higher-levels of performance and help the team to focus on creating high-value Increments that meet the Definition of Done.

Scrum Team

A collection of individuals consisting of one Scrum Master, one Product Owner and Developers. They are self-managing, cross-functional and fewer than ten people. There is no hierarchy in the Scrum Team; it operates as a horizontal structure.

Scrum Values

A statement of ethics for Scrum Teams; the key components of Scrum Values are Courage, Commitment, Focus, Openness and Respect. These behaviours underpin the Scrum framework. One of the central tasks for a Scrum Master (see Scrum Master) is to remind the Scrum Team of the Scrum Values and to reinforce their adoption.

Self-Managing

The autonomous structure of Scrum Teams that allows them to choose how to best accomplish their work and turn Increments into potentially releasable products. Self-managing Scrum Teams actively experiment with approaches, learn from challenges and continuously adapt.

Sprint

A container for the other four Scrum events, this is a short, timeboxed event (typically one month or less) during which a defined set of activities take place and at the end, a product Increment is delivered. Please refer to Figure 10.3 for further information.

Sprint Backlog

During Sprint Planning (see Sprint Planning), the Developers select the Product Backlog items that will best meet the Sprint Goal and place these on the Sprint

Backlog. The Developers identify the tasks necessary to complete each Sprint Backlog item.

Sprint Goal

A Sprint Goal is a short sentence that describes, in holistic terms, what the Scrum Team plans to achieve during the Sprint. It is written collaboratively by the whole Scrum Team. It is the Scrum Master's responsibility to coach the Scrum Team on how to craft a Sprint Goal that is meaningful, not too big, and not too vague. The Sprint Goal must be finalised prior to the end of Sprint Planning.

Sprint Planning

This event takes place at the beginning of each Sprint and is attended by everyone in the Scrum Team. Its purpose is to determine what should be built, how it should be built and why it should be built. Other people from outside the Scrum Team may be invited to provide advice or assist with conveying how the Product Backlog items map to the Product Goal. The Scrum Master coaches the Scrum Team to keep the event within the timebox, which is typically eight hours for a one-month Sprint, or less for shorter Sprints.

Sprint Retrospective

This event takes place at the end of each Sprint and is an opportunity for the Scrum Team to inspect its elf and identify opportunities to improve quality and effectiveness. High-impact improvements should be implemented as soon as possible and can even be added to the upcoming Sprint Backlog. It is timeboxed to a maximum of three hours for a one-month Sprint, or less for shorter Sprints.

Sprint Review

The purpose of the Sprint Review is to inspect what was achieved during the Sprint and to collaborate and agree on the next steps. The Product Owner updates the Product Backlog to reflect new opportunities. Similarly to the other events, The Scrum Master's role is to ensure the event takes place, within the allotted timebox, and that attendees understand its purpose.

Stakeholder

Anyone with a vested interest in the product who is not part of the Scrum Team. This may include end users, project sponsors and subject-matter experts. They typically tend to be invited by the Scrum Team to attend Sprint Planning and the Sprint Review.

PART 11

Practice PSM I Assessment

Set yourself up for success by taking this practice PSM I assessment.

The sample 25 questions are a good way to gauge your current knowledge of Scrum as per the 2020 version of the Scrum Guide™.

These questions have been carefully designed to challenge your awareness and understanding of the Scrum Guide™ and to help you to prepare for the actual PSM I assessment and the tricky questions that are asked.

Good luck!

The Open Assessments do not have the same level of difficulty as the certification assessments.

-SCRUM.ORG

63

PSM I Open Assessment Questions

The sample questions covered in this section are based loosely on the Scrum Open Assessment questions from Scrum.org. Although the questions are similar to those of the actual PSM I assessment, they do not represent the full range of content or levels of difficulty presented in the exam itself.

Some individuals who have taken the actual PSM I assessment have gone on to state on the Scrum.org forum that they found the PSM I Open Assessment questions much easier in comparison to the actual PSM I assessment.

The wording of the questions has been adapted slightly so as to not constitute an infringement of Scrum.org's copyright, as well as to ensure you experience the full breadth of the trickier types of questions that were covered in Part 8.

The questions are broken down into four areas:

- The Scrum Framework;
- Scrum Theory and Principles;
- Cross-Functional, Self-Managing Teams;
- Coaching & Facilitation.

This practice test contains 25 questions but the actual PSM I test will contain 80 questions.

Whilst I have included the detailed answers at the bottom of each page, I strongly recommend you attempt to take the test without reading these to see how well you perform.

Only once you've taken the test should you go back to the beginning and read both the question and the answer together to check your understanding and identify any gaps in your knowledge.

It won't hurt to take the test a few times; leave a few days in between attempts to see if you are absorbing and retaining the information.

64

The Scrum Framework

Question 1

The Scrum Team consists of three types of professionals, with each one having clear accountabilities. From the accountabilities listed below, which three do not form part of the Scrum Team?

Choose from the following:

A. Senior Stakeholders

B. Product Owner

C. External Customers

D. Developers

E. Scrum Master

F. Testers

TIP

Read the question twice before you mark the answers. Keep your eyes open for the words like NOT and NEVER. Some questions specify you to select multiple answers – Select 2, Select 3 etc – so be observant, especially towards the end of the assessment when your focus would naturally tend to drift.

Answer Explained

The Scrum Guide™ states that the Scrum Team consists of one *Product Owner* (responsible for maximising the value of the product), the *Developers* (responsible for delivering a potentially releasable Increment) and one *Scrum Master* (responsible for the Scrum Teams effectiveness). Therefore, the correct answer is - A, C and F.

Collectively, these accountabilities are known as the Scrum Team.

The accountabilities in Scrum are quite different from the roles associated with traditional project delivery teams. Having clearly defined accountabilities and expectations can assist individuals to perform their tasks more efficiently. Each accountability complements the others and success with Scrum can only truly be realised when a Scrum Team embraces all three.

Question 2

The Product Owner is one person and not a committee. From the four statements below, which statement best conveys the responsibilities of the Product Owner in Scrum?

Choose from the following:

A. Directing the Developers on how to complete the work

B. Ensuring that stakeholders are kept away from the Developers

C. Managing the project and ensuring that the work meets stakeholder expectations

D. Doing everything possible to optimise the value of work produced by the Scrum Team

TIP

Use your time wisely. Whilst it's an open assessment, during the exam don't try to Google (or Bing) around for the answers. Firstly, you won't necessarily find any and secondly, there is no guarantee that the answer you find is right. Thirdly, you would be wasting your time. Keep in mind that you need to complete 80 questions in 60 minutes. That gives you just 45 seconds per question – so you need to be fast!

Answer Explained

At the most basic level, a Product Owner is the person responsible for maximising the value of the product produced by the Scrum Team, that's not to say the Developers can't assist with this. The Product Owner is essentially the main bridge between the stakeholders and the Developers. Therefore, the correct answer is – D. Whilst you could argue that some of the other answer options are also relevant, remember the question is asking for the BEST answer to the question.

The Scrum Guide™ states that the Product Owner is accountable for effective Product Backlog management, which includes:

- Developing and explicitly communicating the Product Goal;
- Creating and clearly communicating Product Backlog items;
- Ordering Product Backlog items; and,
- Ensuring that the Product Backlog is transparent, visible and understood.

Question 3

There is often confusion around the role that management plays in Scrum. From the options below, please select the statement you feel best describes the role that management should play in Scrum.

Choose from the following:

A. With any organisation implementing Scrum, the management team play an active role in coaching and supporting the Product Owner with the delivery of a product that delivers value to the customer. In addition, they also assist the Scrum Master with instilling a culture that promotes self-management and empiricism

B. Track, monitor and report on staffing levels, making sure the Scrum Team size is always 10 or fewer people

C. Continually watch the Scrum Team closely and remove people from the team who aren't performing at their highest productivity level after giving them several warnings

D. Absolutely nothing; management don't have a role to play in Scrum

TIP

The more information, the better. More often than not, the correct answer usually contains more information than the other options. This is good to know if you are stuck, pressed for time and need to make a guess.

Answer Explained

Not all companies need managers or have a management team, so there is no real reason for Scrum to comment on the role of a 'manager'. The Scrum Guide™ therefore does not directly address the role of managers in Scrum.

Whilst the management team does not form part of the Scrum Team, it's important for the management team to remember that they still have an important role to play as there are plenty of opportunities to add value to a Scrum Team through supporting the Product Owner and the Scrum Master. Therefore, the correct answer is – A.

Working externally to the Scrum Team, the management team can still support the Product Owner by providing information and strategies to maximise the value of the product. They can also support the Scrum Master to impact organisational change in a way that enables the organisation to successfully adopt Scrum.

Question 4

The entire Scrum Team are accountable for delivering a potentially shippable product that meets the definition of 'Done'. Based on this, what is the recommended size for a Scrum Team in terms of number of people?

Choose from the following:

A. 7 plus or minus 2

B. Minimum of 3 and a maximum of 9

C. It doesn't matter

D. 10 or fewer people

TIP

Answer the questions you know first. If you're having difficulty answering a question, move on and come back to tackle it once you've answered all the questions you know. Sometimes answering easier questions first can offer insight into answering the more challenging questions later.

Answer Explained

According to the Scrum Guide™, the essence of Scrum is a small team of people.

The Scrum Guide™ then goes on to state that the optimal Scrum Team size is: small enough to remain nimble and large enough to complete significant work within a Sprint, typically ten or fewer people. Smaller teams tend to communicate better and are more productive. Therefore, the correct answer is - D.

However, if a Scrum Team is too small, the team may encounter constraints around skills and expertise during the Sprint, and therefore may be unable to deliver a potentially releasable Increment. On the other hand, having more than ten members requires too much coordination. Large Scrum Teams tend to generate too much complexity for an empirical process to be effective.

Question 5

There are lots of different ways to describe Scrum, but which statement below describes Scrum best?

Choose from the following:

A. A predictive and well-defined process that conforms to the principles of Scientific Management

B. A complete methodology that prescribes how to develop a product step-by-step

C. A framework for creating complex products in complex environments

D. A cookbook that defines best practices and principles for product development

E. A sequential set of steps needed to deliver a product at the end of a Sprint

TIP

Read every answer option prior to choosing a final answer. This may seem like a no-brainer to some, but it is a common mistake people make. As I pointed out in the Part 8, there is usually a best answer to every multiple-choice question. If you quickly assume you know the correct answer, without first reading every answer option, you may end up not selecting the best answer.

Answer Explained

First and foremost, Scrum is not a process, technique, or definitive method. Rather, it is a framework within which you can employ various processes and techniques. The Scrum Guide™ alludes to Scrum being a lightweight framework that helps people, teams and organisations generate value through adaptive solutions for complex problems.

Scrum is often confused for being a methodology when it's actually a part of a much broader methodology - Agile; a collection of frameworks and practices that share the same iterative approach to project management and software development.

Scrum wouldn't make a good process because it doesn't define everything you need in order to succeed. Therefore, the correct answer is - C.

Question 6

Each of the five events in Scrum has a timebox. What is the timebox for the Daily Scrum?

Choose from the following:

A. 15 minutes

B. 15 minutes for a 2-week Sprint. For shorter Sprints it is usually shorter

C. Depends on the team size

D. Five minutes per person

E. In the morning of each day of the Sprint

TIP

Don't second guess yourself. It's usually best to stick with your first choice having read all of the answers available! It is often counterproductive to constantly second guess yourself and change your answer. However, this doesn't mean your first answer choice is necessarily the correct choice. While multiple choice tests aren't usually intentionally designed to trick or confuse people, they are designed test a person's knowledge and ability. To this end, the answer options provided will often include the most common wrong answer.

Answer Explained

The Daily Scrum is a 15-minute timeboxed event for the Developers. Therefore, the correct answer is - A.

Timeboxing is a time management tool that allocates a fixed time period, called a timebox, to an activity. Timeboxing is generally used for ensuring that effort is spent economically on an activity and time is not wasted. It keeps the discussion brisk but relevant. As a Scrum Master, timeboxing should already be a part of your toolkit.

Do not be aggressive in timeboxing a particular discussion that the Developers may be engaged in. Sometimes they may be 'in the zone' and a shorter duration may end up doing more damage than good.

Question 7

The Daily Scrum is held at the same time and same place every day. Why is this?

Choose from the following:

A. It makes the process of booking rooms easier

B. The consistency reduces complexity

C. Management demands it so that they can better manage their diaries

D. It makes it easier for the Product Owner to manage their time across multiple projects

TIP

Select the best answer: It's important to select the best answer to the question being asked, not just the answer that seems correct. Often many answers will seem correct, but there is typically a best answer to the question.

Answer Explained

The Daily Scrum is an informal meeting and not a status update meeting for Management. If executed correctly, the Daily Scrum would provide very little benefit to Management; its single purpose is to serve and benefit the Developers.

The Product Owner does not play an active role in the Daily Scrum unless they are playing a dual role of Product Owner and a Developer. The same applies to the Scrum Master.

Having the Daily Scrum at the same time and place probably would make it easier for some Scrum Teams to book meeting rooms, but this wouldn't necessarily be the case for all Scrum Teams.

By holding the Daily Scrum at the same place and time, complexity and uncertainty are reduced. Therefore, the correct answer is - B. The same should be applied across all Scrum events. It is common practice to have the Daily Scrum in the morning, or as soon as the Developers are gathered so that the team may plan and synchronise their activities for the day ahead.

Question 8

A Scrum Master is present at the Daily Scrum. What is the main purpose for the Scrum Master being present?

Choose from the following:

A. To gather the status from the Developers and report this information to management

B. To write down any changes to the Sprint Backlog, including the addition of any new items, and tracking the progress of the Developers

C. He or she does not have to be there; the Scrum Master only has to ensure the Developers have a Daily Scrum and that it is positive, productive and kept within the timebox

D. To make sure every Developer takes part and answers three questions

E. To provide the Developers with light snacks and refreshments

TIP

Make an educated guess: Generally speaking, if it will not count against your score, make an educated guess concerning any question you're unsure about. However, before doing so it is still a good idea to eliminate at least one or two answers that you know to be incorrect before making your guess.

Answer Explained

As previously mentioned, the Daily Scrum is not a status update meeting.

The Scrum Master ensures that the Developers hold the Daily Scrum and that it is productive, positive and kept to the timebox. They do not have to be there. The Scrum Guide™ states that the Developers can choose how to best run the Daily Scrum so long as it focuses on progress towards the Sprint Goal. Some Scrum Teams prefer to use the 'three questions approach' whereby each team member discusses what they did yesterday, what they are planning to do today and whether or not they have any impediments that put the Sprint Goal at risk. The use of these three questions was a format used in previous editions of the Scrum Guide™ and was removed as the recommended format for the Daily Scrum so as to encourage the Scrum Team to self-manage and explore alternative formats. Therefore, the correct answer is – C.

Question 9

The single objective of the Sprint is for the Scrum Team to meet the Sprint Goal.

True or False?

A. True

B. False

TIP

Use your imagination. If after your very best efforts, you cannot choose between two answers, try vividly imagining each one as the correct answer. If you are like most people, you will often 'feel' that one of the answers is wrong. Trust this feeling. Research suggests that feelings are frequently accessible even when recall is poor. For example, we can still know how we feel about a person even when we can't remember the person's name!

Answer Explained

Each Sprint can be looked at as a mini project; much like projects, a Sprint has a goal to accomplish.

The Sprint Goal is the single objective for the Sprint. The Sprint Goal is created during Sprint Planning and then added to the Sprint Backlog. As the Developers work during the Sprint, they keep the Sprint Goal in mind. Therefore, the correct answer is – A.

Question 10

The Developers should not be interrupted by anyone outside of the Scrum Team during the Sprint. The Sprint Goal should remain intact throughout the Sprint. These are conditions that foster productivity, creativity and quality.

Based on the above statement, which one of the following is FALSE?

A. The Developers may negotiate with the Product Owner to add or remove work in the Sprint if it finds it has more or less capacity than expected

B. When invited to do so by the Developers, the Product Owner can help clarify or optimise the Sprint

C. The Sprint Backlog may grow as more becomes known throughout the Sprint and new work emerges

D. The Sprint Backlog is fixed during the Sprint Planning session and is not allowed to be altered during the Sprint

TIP

Accept the question at face value. Read the questions and the language used carefully, but don't assume the question is trying to trick you. Reading too much into a question can result in you selecting the wrong answer.

Answer Explained

As new work is required, the Developers add it to the Sprint Backlog.

As work is performed or completed during the Sprint, the estimated remaining work is updated in the Sprint Backlog. When elements of the plan are deemed unnecessary, they are removed. Only the Developers can change the Sprint Backlog during a Sprint.

The Sprint Backlog *does change* and is updated during the Sprint. Therefore, the correct answer is - D.

Question 11

Although not common, in some Scrum Teams a Sprint may be cancelled before the timebox is reached. When might a Sprint be cancelled?

Choose from the following:

A. When the marketing department has an important new opportunity that requires the attention of the Scrum Team

B. When the Product Owner deems the Sprint Goal to be obsolete

C. When it becomes apparent that not everything will be finished in time by the end of the Sprint

D. When the Developers reach the consensus that the work is too difficult for them to complete

TIP

Try to supply your own answer before reading the options provided. Read the question while covering the choices provided with your hand. Try to answer the question yourself then read through the available answers. Doing this allows you to make a more accurate choice.

Answer Explained

Only the Product Owner has the authority to cancel the Sprint, although he or she may do so under direction and influence from the Scrum Master, the Developers or even other people in the organisation. The Product Owner can cancel a Sprint at any point before the Sprint timebox is reached.

A Sprint would be cancelled in the event that the Sprint Goal became obsolete. This could occur for a number of reasons, for example, if the company chooses to change direction or if market or technology conditions suddenly change. In general, due to the short duration of Sprints, cancellation rarely makes sense and most Product Owners choose to continue with the Sprint.

When a Sprint is cancelled, any completed Product Backlog items are reviewed by the Product Owner and if the Product Owner sees that part of the work is potentially releasable, they generally tend to accept it. All incomplete Product Backlog Items are re-estimated and put back on the Product Backlog. The decision to cancel a Sprint should not be taken lightly as Sprint cancellation consumes resources and takes time to re-plan. Therefore, Sprint cancellations are not commonplace in Scrum Teams. Therefore, the correct answer is - B.

Question 12

The Product Increment is the sum of the Product Backlog items completed during a Sprint and the value of the Increments of all previous Sprints.

True or false? It is mandatory that the product Increment be released into production at the end of each Sprint for the customer to start benefiting as soon as possible.

A. True

B. False

TIP

Leave enough time. Be sure to leave enough time at the end of your exam to check your answers and revisit the questions that you found too difficult to answer first time around and answer them.

Answer Explained

During the Sprint, the new Increment must be 'Done,' which means it must be in a useable condition and meet the Scrum Team's definition of 'Done.'

A product Increment is a body of inspectable, done work that supports empiricism at the end of the Sprint. The Increment is a step towards a vision or goal.

The Increment must be in a useable condition regardless of whether the Product Owner decides to release it into production or not, therefore an Increment doesn't have to be released into production as part of each Sprint.

The Scrum Guide™ states that the purpose of each Sprint is to deliver Increments of potentially releasable functionality that adhere to the Scrum Team's current definition of 'Done.' The key word here is *potentially.* Therefore, the correct answer is - B.

Question 13

The Developers come to the realisation that they will not be able to complete the forecasted items on the Sprint Backlog during the Sprint, putting the Sprint Goal in jeopardy. A meeting is called to revise the Sprint work selected. Who should be present at the meeting?

Choose from the following:

A. The Scrum Team

B. The Developers and the Scrum Master

C. The Product Owner and the Developers

D. The Product Owner and Project Stakeholders

TIP

Look for the answers in the rest of the exam. Read through the wording of questions and see if anything in there will help you answer the question you're stuck on. While it probably won't be explicitly mentioned anywhere, you might get lucky and find a familiar term to jog your memory. It is only recommended you do this if you have time available to do so.

Answer Explained

As the Developers work together, they keep the Sprint Goal in mind. If the Developers discover that the work is different to what they anticipated, they collaborate with the Product Owner to review the scope of Sprint Backlog. Therefore, only the Product Owner and the Developers are required at the meeting.

The Product Owner is there to help answer questions about the selected Product Backlog Items and work with the Developers on what is achievable. If the Developers decide that they have either too much or too little work to do, they may renegotiate the selected Product Backlog items with the Product Owner. Therefore, the correct answer is – C.

Question 14

The Product Backlog is a prioritised list of work for the Developers to build a shippable product. What is the Product Backlog ordered by?

Choose from the following:

A. Size, where small items of work are at the top and larger items are at the bottom

B. There is no order; items are randomly arranged

C. Risk, where the safer known items are at the top, and the riskier items are at the bottom

D. Least valuable items at the top to most valuable at the bottom

E. Whatever is deemed most appropriate by the Product Owner

TIP

Go with your gut feeling. Usually there are a few possible answers and some that are just plain laughable; use your common sense and go with your gut, the answer is there somewhere!

Answer Explained

The Product Backlog is an ordered list of everything that is known to be required to reach a finished product. It is the single source of truth for everything that is required to deliver the product to the customer.

The Product Backlog is a living artefact; it constantly evolves to identify what the product needs to remain relevant, competitive, and useful to the customer. The Product Backlog typically contains a set of features, functions, requirements, enhancements, and fixes. Product Backlog items include a description, are ordered, estimated, and have a perceived value. In addition, items often include test descriptions that will evidence the product's completeness when 'Done.'

The Product Owner is accountable for the Product Backlog, including the availability of items, the content contained within the items and of course, the ordering of items by whatever the Product Owner deems to be of the most value. Therefore, the correct answer is – E.

Question 15

The Scrum Team could choose to take the highest-priority changes to improve its effectiveness, identified during the Sprint Retrospective, and address these as soon as possible or place these in the Sprint Backlog to be considered as part of the next Sprint.

True or False?

A. True

B. False

TIP

Try certainty marking. You should be answering all the questions that you know are right, so if you answer a question you are certain you got right then put a tick next to the question number. Marking the questions will help you keep track of what needs to be answered if you have time later in the test.

Answer Explained

During the Sprint Retrospective, the Scrum Team identifies elements of the Sprint that did or did not work, along with potential solutions. Sprint Retrospectives help the team to gather each other's feedback and create an action plan for improving effectiveness.

Sprint Retrospectives mark the end of a Sprint. They usually happen after the Sprint Review and before the next Sprint Planning.

By the end of the Sprint Retrospective, the Scrum Team should have identified improvements that it will implement as part of the next Sprint, or sooner. Although improvements may be implemented by the Scrum Team at any point in time, and the sooner the better, the Sprint Retrospective provides a more formal setting for the Scrum Team to focus their efforts on inspecting and adapting their processes.

An experienced Scrum Master is essential for a successful Sprint Retrospective. While there are many ways to identify issues, it is the Scrum Master's responsibility to facilitate the Sprint Retrospective so that the Scrum Team identifies true process issues and develops actionable solutions in line with the Agile principles. Therefore, the correct answer is – A.

Question 16

A Sprint Backlog is the set of items that cross-functional Scrum Teams select from the Product Backlog to work on during the Sprint. When does a Developer become the sole owner of a Sprint Backlog item?

Choose from the following:

A. At the first Daily Scrum of the Sprint

B. Never. All Sprint Backlog items 'owned' by all of the Developers, even though each one may be worked on by an individual Developer

C. At the point when a particular team member can accommodate more work

D. During Sprint Planning

TIP

Make sure you leave yourself enough time to review your answers before you submit them at the end as you might have had something else in the test jog your mind or the answer might seem a little clearer after you have worked on the test. The trick is to go back and read over everything so you are giving yourself the best chance at answering everything correctly.

Answer Explained

As new work is required and realised during the Sprint to reach the Sprint Goal, the Developers add it to the Sprint Backlog. As work is performed or completed, the estimated remaining work on the Sprint Backlog is updated.

When elements of the Sprint Backlog are deemed unnecessary, they are simply removed. Only the Developers can change their Sprint Backlog during a Sprint. The Scrum Master and Product Owner are not allowed to alter the Sprint Backlog.

The items on the Sprint Backlog belong to all of the Developers. Therefore, the correct answer is - B.

Question 17

The definition of 'Done' is an agreed upon list of the items or activities necessary to get a product Increment to a 'Done' state during a Sprint. Who is responsible for agreeing the Definition of Done?

Choose from the following:

A. The Product Owner as he/she is responsible for the success of the product

B. The Developers

C. If one does not already exist for the organisation, then the Scrum Team

D. The Scrum Master as he/she is the custodian of the framework and therefore best placed

E. The Developers and the Product Owner

TIP

Take a constructive approach. It's been shown that when you carry extra emotional baggage -- 'I've got to ace this exam' or 'If I screw up, I'll never get that promotion' -- performance suffers. The most constructive approach is to focus on the task at hand, put in as much time studying as you can afford, and just do your best.

Answer Explained

The Definition of Done is crucial to a Scrum Team. Those performing the work (the Developers) and those inspecting the resulting Increment (the Product Owner) must share a common Definition of Done - this helps with transparency.

The Definition of Done is an agreement between the Developers and the Product Owner on what needs to be completed for each user story - and it is often standardised across the company in order to guarantee consistent delivery of quality across multiple teams. Therefore, the correct answer is - C.

Question 18

In the event that multiple Scrum Teams are working on building a single product, how is the Definition of Done handled?

Choose from the following:

A. All Scrum Teams must have a Definition of Done that make their combined work potentially releasable

B. Each Scrum Team defines and uses its own Definition of Done that makes sense to them. The differences across the various definitions are shared amongst the Scrum Teams and addressed closer to the completion of the product

C. Each Scrum Team uses its own definition but must make their definition clear to all other teams so the differences are known for transparency purposes

D. None of the above

TIP

This is a process of elimination. Once you're sure you know what the question is asking, you should begin by eliminating any answer choices that you know to be incorrect. This will allow you to focus on the remaining answers. Not only will this strategy save you time but it greatly increases your likelihood of selecting the correct answer.

Answer Explained

Multiple Scrum Teams often work on the same product together. According to the Scrum Guide™, one Product Backlog is used to describe the upcoming work on the product. There will also be one Product Owner.

If there are multiple Scrum Teams working on the system or product release, the Developers across all the Scrum Teams must mutually define the 'Definition of Done'. Therefore, the correct answer is - A.

Question 19

Each Scrum Team should always have a separate Product Backlog that they maintain independently of other Scrum Teams, even when working on the same product.

True or False?

A. True

B. False

TIP

Pay particularly close attention to the words 'not', 'sometimes', 'always', and 'never'. An answer that includes 'always' must be irrefutable. If you can find a single counter example, then the answer is not correct. The same holds true for the word 'never'. If an answer option includes 'never' a single counter example will likely indicate the answer is not correct.

Answer Explained

If a Scrum Team becomes too large, making coordination difficult, simply form more teams.

For larger projects, multiple Scrum Teams often work together on the same product. If there are multiple teams working on the same product, they will need to work from a single Product Backlog describing the upcoming work on the product.

Even though the Scrum Teams all work from the main Product Backlog, they still maintain their own individual team Sprint Backlogs and Scrum events such as the Daily Scrum. Multiple Product Backlogs for the same product are not necessary.

If there are dependencies on other Scrum Teams' requirements, this affects the prioritisation: for example, a requirement might be placed further towards the bottom of the list in accordance with its business value. But because another Scrum Team depends on its implementation, it moves further towards the top of the Product Backlog. Therefore, the correct answer is – B.

65

Scrum Theory and Principles

Question 20

Scrum is founded on a particular type of process control, but which one?

Choose from the following:

A. Quality

B. Complexity

C. Empirical

D. Strategic

TIP

Find a balance. There's no need to go all 'Need for Speed' during your exam. However, don't be as slow as a sloth. Find the right balance and you should be okay. This can be done by practicing on Scrum open assessments. By working at a steady pace, you won't panic. When you panic, your brain joins in, making it harder to recall information that you've spent time learning.

Answer Explained

In Scrum, decisions are made based on observation and experimentation rather than on detailed upfront planning.

Scrum is founded on empirical process control theory, or empiricism.

Empiricism asserts that knowledge comes from experience and making decisions based on what is known. Scrum employs an iterative, incremental approach to optimise predictability and control risk. Therefore, the correct answer is – C.

Question 21

Empirical process control relies on the three main pillars. What are the three pillars?

Choose from the following:

A. Planning, Review, Retrospective

B. Transparency, Inspection, Adaptation

C. Respect, Commitment, Courage

D. Transparency, Planning, Inspection

TIP

Remember that each question only carries one mark. If you're unable to solve a particular question don't waste too much time on it. You can always bookmark the difficult questions and try to answer these at a later point during the assessment, perhaps after completing the easier questions. There is absolutely no reason to answer the questions in the order they appear in the exam. It is up to you if you would like to approach answering the easiest questions first before returning to the more challenging questions. Sometimes answering easier questions first can offer insight into answering the more challenging questions later.

Answer Explained

Three pillars uphold every implementation of empirical process control: transparency, inspection, and adaptation. Therefore, the correct answer is - B.

Significant aspects of the process must be visible to those responsible for the outcome. Transparency requires those aspects be defined by a common standard so observers share a common understanding of what is being seen.

Scrum Team members must frequently inspect Scrum artefacts and progress toward a Sprint Goal to detect undesirable variances. Their inspection should not be so frequent that inspection gets in the way of the work. An adaptation must be made as soon as possible to minimise further deviation.

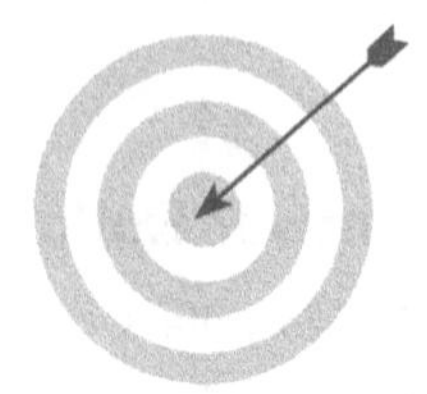

66

Cross-Functional, Self-Managing Teams

Question 22

In some circumstances, the Developers on a Scrum Team should change. Under what circumstances should this occur?

Choose from the following:

A. As required, while taking into account a short-term reduction in team productivity

B. As required, with no special allowance for changes in team productivity

C. Every other Sprint to increase knowledge across the team and organisation

D. Never, because it reduces the productivity of the team

TIP

Read look-alike answer options judiciously. If two of the alternatives are similar, one is likely to be correct; choose the best but eliminate choices that mean basically the same thing, and thus cancel each other out.

Answer Explained

Once you have the right people on board, minimise any changes to the Scrum Team within and across major releases. It takes time for a group of individuals to become a true Scrum Team; a tightly knit unit with members that trust and support each other and that work together well. Changing the Scrum Team composition too frequently is not desirable. Teams need stability to flourish and realise their full potential.

Try to keep teams together. Don't make frequent changes in teams. New Scrum Teams take time to learn to work together; therefore, making frequent changes (even between projects) adds time for the team to learn to work together. Therefore, the correct answer is – A.

Question 23

Which three behaviours demonstrate that a Scrum Team is not self-managing and not adhering to Scrum as per the Scrum Guide™?

Choose the best three answers from the following:

A. The Developers have all the skills needed to create a releasable Increment

B. Management attend the Daily Scrum to check on the progress of the Developers and remaining scope for the Sprint to see if they complete it sooner

C. The Developers devise their own Sprint Backlog, reflecting all work that meets the definition of 'Done'

D. The Developers collaboratively discussing and selecting their own work during the Sprint

E. The Developers inviting people from outside the Scrum Team to the Sprint Planning to ask them how to turn a Product Backlog item into an Increment via a complete and detailed Sprint Backlog

F. The Developers are working within the boundaries of their functional description and nicely handing-off work from Tester to Developer to Integration and back to Analyst

TIP

Always provide an answer. The PSM I does not penalise you for incorrect answers, by that I mean you do not lose additional marks for getting a question wrong – you simply don't get awarded the mark for the question. Answering a question is always better than not. If you don't know the answer, try to make a guess.

Answer Explained

The Developers should have all the skills between them to create a releasable Increment. They are also responsible for making their own decisions about how best to approach their work. In addition, they also have a strong willingness to cooperate with each other. Therefore, the correct answer is – B, E & F.

Question 24

In order for the Developers to have success with Scrum, what should they become more proficient with?

Choose from the following:

A. Living the five Scrum values

B. Completing all items on the Product Backlog and essentially closing the project

C. Transforming the items, it selects for the Sprint Backlog into an Increment of potentially releasable product functionality

TIP

Don't get distracted. Remember, if three answer choices are presented, two of them are incorrect. They are called distractors for good reason. Often, distractors are written to appear correct at first glance.

Answer Explained

In order for the Developers to have success with Scrum, they should become more proficient with the five Scrum values. Therefore, the correct answer is – A.

In addition, Developers should have the following characteristics:

- Be self-managing. No one should dictate to the Developers how they should approach the Product Backlog in order to turn it into Increments of potentially releasable functionality. The Developers can ask for support from the Product Owner, the Scrum Master as well as others only if needed;
- Be cross-functional. The Developers should have all the skills necessary to create a Product Increment
- Scrum recognises no sub-teams in the Scrum Team, regardless of domains that need to be addressed like testing, architecture, operations, or business analysis; and,
- Individual Developers may have specialised skills and areas of focus, but accountability belongs to the Scrum Team as a whole.

67

Coaching and Facilitation

Question 25

An organisation is keen to implement Scrum. However, the management team want to change the terminology used in Scrum to fit with terminology already used elsewhere in the organisation. If this was to happen, how would this impact their success with Scrum?

Choose from the following:

A. Without a new vocabulary to serve as a reminder of the change, very little change may actually happen

B. The organisation may not be able to clearly see what has changed following the implementation of Scrum and therefore the benefits of Scrum maybe lost entirely

C. Employees will likely feel less anxious with adopting Scrum

D. All of the above

TIP

'All of the above' and 'None of the above'. When you encounter 'All of the above' and 'None of the above' answer choices, do not select 'All of the above' if you are pretty sure any one of the answers provided is incorrect. The same applies for 'None of the above' if you are confident that at least one of the answer choices is true. It sounds obvious but you'd be surprised at the difficulty some people have with these types of questions.

Answer Explained

A common language referring to the process must be shared by all participants for Scrum to be successful. Without the incorporation of the official Scrum Glossary, the organisation may not understand what has actually changed with adopting Scrum and the benefits of Scrum may be lost. Without a new vocabulary to remind people in the organisation of the change, very little change may occur. The management will likely feel less anxious as without the introduction of a new vocabulary, not much will change. Therefore, the correct answer is - D.

Table 11.1 Practice PSM I Assessment Answers

Practice PSM I Assessment	
Questions & Answers	
Area: The Scrum Framework	1. A, C & F 2. D 3. A 4. D 5. C 6. A 7. B 8. C 9. A 10. D 11. B 12. B 13. C 14. E 15. A 16. B 17. C 18. A 19. B
Area: Scrum Theory & Principles	20. C 21. B
Area: Cross-Functional, Self-Managing Teams	22. A 23. B, E & F 24. A
Area: Coaching & Facilitation	25. D

Nothing is impossible.
The word itself says 'I'm possible'.

-AUDREY HEPBURN

PART 12
Study Guide

I'm sure you've heard of the phrase 'failing to prepare is like preparing to fail'. You can work hard to learn large quantities of information for an exam, but if you don't prepare yourself mentally and physically before the exam, all that hard work can potentially go to waste.

To succeed in passing your PSM I, you should allocate enough study time to prepare effectively. The suggestions over the next few pages contain all of the important information you will need in order to study for the assessment and should be treated as your roadmap to PSM I success!

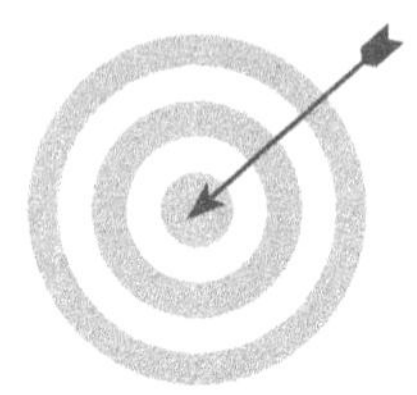

68

Gather Study Materials

It's important to gather all the materials and information that you will need as part of your study programme.

Here is a list of everything you will need:

- A copy of the 2020 Scrum Guide™;
- A copy of the Nexus Framework;
- A copy of the Scrum Glossary (see Part 10 of this book);
- Access to the following open assessments on Scrum.org:
  - Scrum OPEN
  - Nexus OPEN
  - Product Owner OPEN
  - Developer OPEN.

By gathering these materials, you will be able to visualise the bigger picture in terms of all the information you are going to need to consider as part of your study timetable.

69

Allocate Study Time

When it comes to studying for an open-book exam, the most important thing to give yourself is plenty of time. Finding the time to study alongside work and personal commitments can be challenging, but allocating yourself enough time to study is key to achieving the results you want.

It depends on the individual, but generally speaking the average person will need between one to six weeks to prepare for the PSM I assessment.

Work out how much time you can spend studying towards the PSM I each day. It's best to break your study time into short study sessions, for example, 2-hour blocks instead of say, 6 hours, allowing you to focus your time on the areas of the PSM I assessment you find the most difficult. By doing this you will increase your productivity and limit your chances of burning out!

70

Create Study Environment

Studying at home is the most convenient option for most, but it can also be the most distracting if you live with other people. Keeping distractions under control can help to sharpen your focus and improve your likelihood of retaining information.

Maybe you'd prefer to study in a library, at the beach, in silence or listening to Taylor Swift? Spend some time figuring out what is going to put you in your most productive state. Being comfortable is important, too, but so is finding a balance - you don't want to be so comfortable that you are falling asleep.

It's sometimes a good idea to experiment with different lighting and room temperatures. Having a room that is too hot, too cold, or too bright can lead to you making more mistakes than you would otherwise.

Follow these four simple steps to create your perfect study environment:

- Remove or limit all distractions;
- Have all of your study materials organised and easily accessible;
- Experiment with the lighting;
- Adjust the room temperature so that it's not too hot and not too cold. As Goldilocks would say, it needs to be 'just right'.

71

Keep it Interesting

Studying can be interesting, as long as you keep some variety in your schedule. Whilst variety may be fairly limited as you're studying just the one subject at the end of the day - Scrum - you can incorporate some variety in terms of styles of learning.

For example, on Mondays you could focus on reading and memorising information, on Tuesdays you could adopt the use of flashcards, on Wednesdays you could draw diagrams to assist with the retaining of information etc. You get the idea.

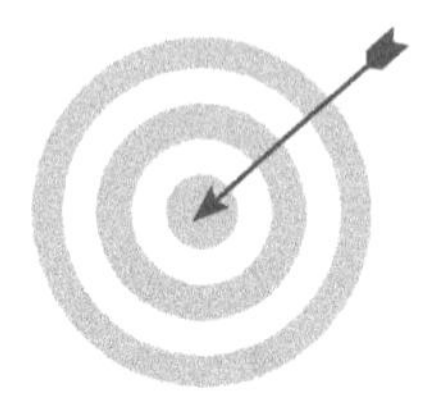

72

Know Why You're Taking the PSM I

It may sound obvious but you need to know why you're taking the PSM I exam if you're going to pour your heart and soul into your revision. This goes beyond the vague idea that you need to pass your exam to get a good Scrum Master job. You need to have a personal reason for getting the best result possible; this in turn will unleash your motivation.

73

Make a Plan

There isn't a set date or time to take the PSM I assessment, which means it's up to you to decide when to schedule your exam. However, it's important that you work towards a fixed date, so that you can build a study schedule around this date.

Once you have set yourself a target date that you're committed to and have an idea of the different areas you would like to focus on to prepare for the assessment, you should make a study schedule. Your study schedule should give you time to take in and process the information.

If you can stick to your study schedule, studying will be more productive. At the end of your first week, inspect what's working and not working so well and adapt your schedule as necessary. Make adjustments for the areas you're struggling with and allocate more time to these.

There is a wide variety of free schedules, planners and time management tools available online, so take some time to research them and choose the one that best meets your needs.

74

Reward Yourself

After each completed study session, be sure to reward yourself: watch Netflix, call your friends, play a game or indulge in some chocolate cake. Have a power nap! Do whatever will motivate you to get through the rest of your study schedule.

75

Stay Healthy

When you are studying, remember to make time for sleeping and exercising. Taking care of your health and well-being will ensure you are in your optimal state, helping to improve your memory, mood and energy levels, and keeping those stress levels down.

You should be aiming to get between 7-9 hours of sleep each night. For the best quality sleep, try to avoid screen-time for at least an hour before bedtime and caffeine for at least 4-6 hours, and give yourself a bit of time to unwind before bedtime. If you've tried these things and still can't sleep, leave your room and do something relaxing until you begin to feel tired.

Drinking plenty of water, eating three meals, and sticking to healthy snacks throughout the day will give your body the fuel it needs to focus. If you're feeling a bit lethargic, try stepping outside for some fresh air. A good goal is to aim for 20-30 minutes of exercise each day, but even a brisk walk around the block between study sessions will do you the world of good and increase your study stamina.

76

Study at the Right Time

We all have our daily highs and lows. Some people focus best at night and are nocturnal, while some people perform best in the mornings. Take advantage of the time of day when you feel most productive, and don't try to force yourself to study when your brainpower isn't at its peak. It's common sense to try to study when you are most alert, so you are able to process and retain the information that you are learning.

77

Use a Timer

A timer can come in useful and help to keep you on track and to make sure you stick to the study schedule that you created. Setting a timer helps keeps you focused on the task at hand, committed to working until the timer goes off, and helps you cover all the material you need to. Above all else, it helps keep your break time effective and guilt-free (because you've earned it!).

PART 13
Taking the PSM I Assessment

In order to take the PSM I exam you'll need to purchase a password which provides you with access to the PSM I assessment and one attempt at taking the exam. This password is your gateway to the exam. It has no expiration date and is valid for one attempt only.

Purchasing the PSM I password is a fairly easy and intuitive process and takes just a few minutes to do.

Don't forget, if you're taking a training course with Scrum.org and being taught by a Professional Scrum Trainer (PST), you do not need to purchase the PSM I assessment separately, as one attempt at the exam is typically included as part of your training course. Speak to your PST to confirm.

78

PSM I Readiness Checklist

The decision about whether you're ready to take the PSM I assessment can be a hard one to make. So just how do you know when you're ready for the most challenging entry-level Scrum Master exam? At what point can you confidently say to yourself, 'Do your worst, PSM I!'

Well, if you have achieved all of the milestones on the checklist below, this is a good indication that you're ready! The primary purpose of the PSM I Readiness Checklist is to help you to review your readiness for the exam.

PSM I Readiness Checklist

- ☐ I have some degree of experience of acting in the capacity of a Scrum Master, servant-leading and coaching teams and organisations on the Scrum framework.
- ☐ I have read the latest version of the Scrum Guide™ (several times) and fully comprehend the definition of Scrum, including the accountabilities, events and artefacts.
- ☐ I have read the latest version of the Nexus Guide™ (several times) and fully understand how multiple Scrum Teams work together.

- ☐ I have taken all four of the Scrum Open Assessments (Scrum Open, Product Owner Open, Nexus Open and Scrum Developer Open) and have reached a point where I consistently achieve a score of no less than 100% on each open assessment.
- ☐ I have asked all of my questions via the Scrum.org Forum to clarify my understanding in areas and topics I either don't understand or am unsure of.
- ☐ I have familiarised myself with the Glossary of Scrum Terms and can correctly recall and identify every term listed.
- ☐ I have a clear idea as to whether or not I'm aiming for a pass mark of either 85% or 95%, depending on whether or not I want to pursue a career as a Scrum.org Certified Scrum Trainer (CST).
- ☐ I have read and understood the answers given in the practice assessment in Part 11 of this book.
- ☐ I have decided how I am going to reward myself once I've passed the PSM I.
- ☐ I have registered with Scrum.org and purchased the PSM I assessment (if not taking the assessment through a PST).
- ☐ I have read and digested the Tips and Tricks in Part 8 of this book.
- ☐ I have an environment that is free from distractions and has a stable internet connection.
- ☐ I feel confident and ready to take on the PSM I assessment.

People rarely feel 100% ready to take an exam, but if you have ticked all the items on this list, you will be. After that, it all just comes down to two factors: focus and self-belief.

It can be difficult to maintain focus for an extended period of time; getting a good night's sleep the night before you take the exam certainly helps. Drinking water during an exam has also been proven to increase a person's cognitive abilities.

Once you're feeling confident enough to take the assessment, just go for it! To be self-confident is to trust in your own abilities and believe that you can do whatever you set your mind to; just make sure it's set to passing the PSM I before you hit the start button! Mindset is everything.

Whether you think you can,
or whether you think you can't,
you're right.

-HENRY FORD

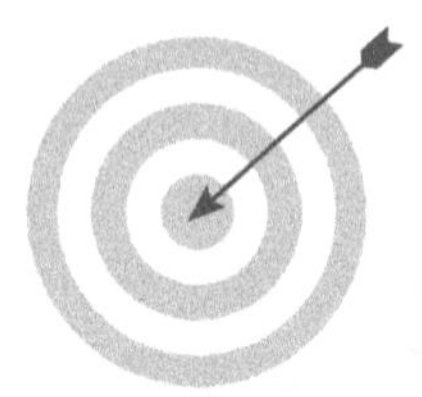

79

Steps to Purchase the PSM I Exam

1 Register with Scrum.org

2 Create Scrum.org Profile

3 Purchase PSM I Assessment

4 Start PSM I Assessment

80

Register with Scrum.org

The first step to purchasing the PSM I assessment is to register with Scrum.org via their website. Visit www.scrum.org and click the 'register' link in the top right-hand corner.

You will be asked to populate the following three fields:

- First name
- Last name
- Email address

Note that your email address will not be made public and needs to be a valid email because this is where you'll receive all future correspondence from Scrum.org, including information about the PSM I assessment.

Although it's not mandatory, you will be asked to say how you heard about Scrum.org and are given a list of options to choose from. Select the option that best applies.

Next, you will need to tick the relevant boxes to confirm that you're not a robot (providing that is, that you're indeed not a robot) and have read and accepted Scrum.org's Terms & Conditions.

Lastly, you will need to click the 'submit' button to send your registration request to Scrum.org.

One of the benefits to registering with Scrum.org is being kept up-to-date on the latest developments in Scrum, as well as Scrum.org specific products, news and events.

- **Complete Your Registration**

  Within just a few minutes of registering you will receive a welcome email to the email address that you provided when you registered. To complete your registration, you will need to click on the 'Complete Registration' link contained within the email. You will then be asked to create a password for your account.

  To complete your registration, simply click 'submit'. It really is as simple as that.

81

Create Scrum.org Profile

Upon completing your registration, you will be redirected to your 'My Scrum.org' account profile.

Your profile is public and allows you to showcase your professional Scrum achievements, and any training that you've invested in, to both current and future employers and clients.

Your name will appear on your public profile by default. There is no option to manually add details of your Scrum.org certifications and any scheduled training courses as this information is automatically pulled from the system and displayed as and when you achieve them.

It is important to make sure that your first name and last name are ordered and spelt correctly, as this is exactly how they will appear on any Scrum.org certifications that you receive.

Note: it may take up to one hour for your assessment result or certification details to show on your Scrum.org profile.

You must have registered with Scrum.org before you can purchase any Professional Scrum Assessments.

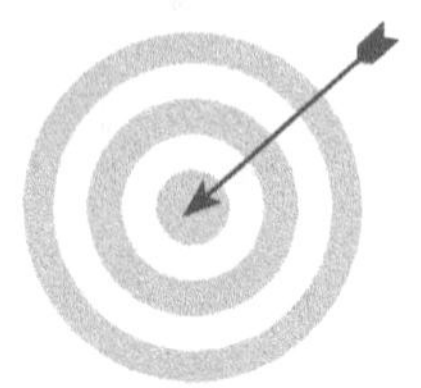

82

Purchase PSM I Assessment

Once you've registered and completed your account profile information, your next step is to actually purchase the PSM I assessment. To do this, navigate your way to the 'Certification' area of the Scrum.org website and select the *Professional Scrum Master*.

Just below the PSM I details, you'll see the option to 'Buy'. Once you've selected buy you'll be redirected to your shopping basket. Follow the on-screen prompts to purchase the assessment.

After you've purchased the assessment, you will receive a confirmation email with a link to download your invoice as a PDF for your records. Your password to access the PSM I will also be emailed to you separately within one business day.

It is then up to you to decide when and where to take the assessment.

83

Start PSM I Assessment

So you've followed the advice and guidance given in this book, you've ticked off all the PSM I Readiness Checklist criteria and now feel ready to take the assessment? That's fantastic!

Go to the email that you received from Scrum.org and copy your assessment password. Next, go to Scrum.org's website and navigate your way to the PSM I assessment page and click 'Start Assessment'. After you've read through the technical consideration, paste your assessment password into the box provided and click 'Start'.

But before you do, please note:

- You cannot save the exam and come back later to finish it;
- If you find that the timer continues to count down but the page is not properly loading during your assessment session, you may find that reloading/refreshing the page can help to resolve this issue;
- When you reach the last question, the *Submit & Forward* button will be replaced by a *Save and Finish* button. Your assessment session will be submitted and graded once you click the Save and Finish button. Be careful not to click Save and Finish if you have bookmarked questions that you need to review before submitting.

- **The best time to purchase the assessment**

  You can purchase the PSM at any time. What's important to understand is there is no set time to take the exam once you have purchased it. The voucher code that you receive doesn't expire. Which raises the question: when is the best time to purchase the exam? In short, it's entirely up to you when you purchase the exam. Some people prefer to do this as early as possible so that they are mentally committed to following through with the assessment. Another good reason for taking this approach is to lock in the purchase price (currently $150 USD) so that in the event that Scrum.org increases the cost of the assessment, you're not impacted financially in between making the decision to take the exam and actually taking the exam. On the other hand, you may prefer to keep your money in your pocket for as long as possible and purchase the exam at the exact point when you are ready to take it.

- **Discounts on the PSM**

  Don't waste time searching for discounts for the PSM I because you won't find any; Scrum.org do not offer discounts on their certifications.

- **Cancellation**

  In order to cancel an order and request a refund for a Scrum.org assessment password, the following two strict conditions must be met:

  - The order must have been placed within the last 60 days;
  - The password must not have been used.

  No cancellations or refunds will be processed for any orders after 60 days from the original purchase date.

- **Completing the assessment**

  Upon completing the exam, your test results will be displayed on your screen and summarised together with a score that is broken down by four subject areas:

- Scrum Framework;
- Scrum Theory & Principles;
- Cross-Functional & Self-Managing Teams;
- Coaching & Facilitation.

You don't need to take a screen-shot; the same results will be sent to the e-mail address that you registered with. It used to be the case that after the exam, you would see a list with wrong answers and correct answers, sometimes with explanation of reasoning behind it. Nowadays you won't see that.

- **Your PSM certification**

  Scrum.org does not send certificates via email, or create or issue hard copies. After logging into Scrum.org, under your profile, you will find the PSM I badge and you can download your Professional Scrum Master I certificate in PDF format, with your name on it.

There is not much more to say on this subject other than to wish you good luck! But seriously, you've got this.

PART 14

Now That You've Passed

After days, weeks or even months of preparing for the PSM I assessment, the moment finally arrives when you pass your exam and become a certified Professional Scrum Master - Level 1 (PSM I) with Scrum.org. Congratulations!

All of your hard work, dedication and commitment have paid off. You should be extremely proud of yourself; passing the PSM I is a huge achievement.

What you choose to do next is entirely up to you, but just in case you're stuck for ideas, this last part lays out some suggestions.

84

Celebrate

No matter the occasion, success deserves acknowledgement.

After what may have felt like an eternity of thinking about taking the PSM I to actually booking the exam, you've done it; you've passed the assessment and are now a qualified Professional Scrum Master with Scrum.org!

First and foremost, you should definitely celebrate this occasion, be it meeting up with friends or going out for dinner with family.

It's really important that you reward yourself for your efforts. This releases pleasure chemicals such as dopamine in your brain, which improves your motivation levels. But remember, 'It's not over until it's over.' Don't start celebrating until you receive the email from Scrum.org confirming that you've passed, but once you do, go ahead and reward yourself - you deserve it!

Have you been eyeing the latest iPhone? Dreaming about upgrading your router? Or maybe you've been drooling over a life-size Avengers statue (collector's edition, of course). Well, don't you think you deserve a little special something after all that time you've put into passing your exam?

I'm the first to admit that nothing I do is ever good enough for me. I constantly have goals, meet them, and immediately move on to the next thing without taking even a moment to acknowledge my success.

So be proud of all that you've accomplished. Celebrate your achievements. You've put in the hard work, and you deserve to feel happy. So many people tell me that they're unwilling to celebrate because they're so focused on the process. Well, before long, if that's the case, you may go a whole lifetime without taking a bow.

If you're unwilling to celebrate your biggest accomplishments, how will you know what the finish line really looks like? Every great venture has both a starting line and a finish line. To begin, you need to be committed. To finish, you need to be consistent. And when you finish, you should celebrate all the hard work, dedication, sweat, tears and energy you've spent on achieving your goal.

85

Better Your Situation

Does achieving your PSM I certification now qualify you for your dream job? Or maybe it now puts you in a stronger position to negotiate a pay increase from your current employer or client?

It's only natural to re-evaluate your career options and current salary package when you achieve a new certification. It's always wise to ask for an increase in your salary when you feel you can justify it, as you'll likely need to put together a strong case.

Choose the right time

Picking the right time is crucial. First thing on a Monday or late on a Friday are considered the worst days to ask. One survey picked out Wednesday as the day on which employers are most likely to be receptive to a pay rise request, but think about the rhythms of your workplace before you decide on the best time. It may be that your boss is always busy, which is usually the case, but don't let that stop you from taking charge of your own future.

Be realistic

Demanding your salary be doubled is unlikely to get you anywhere other than the classifieds looking for a new job. Bear in mind the research you have done into comparable salaries in other organisations, and that your boss does not have to agree to give you any more money. If you want to be listened to and your request taken seriously, you need to pitch it right.

Learn how to negotiate

The key to successful negotiation is good preparation. Be sure of your objective and your arguments, present your case clearly and succinctly and, most of all, don't be afraid of failure and having your request declined.

Have a back-up plan

Just because your boss has turned down a pay increase doesn't mean you can't ask for non-financial benefits as an alternative. It's important to think about what you might accept instead. For example, additional paid annual leave, a higher car allowance or increased training and development.

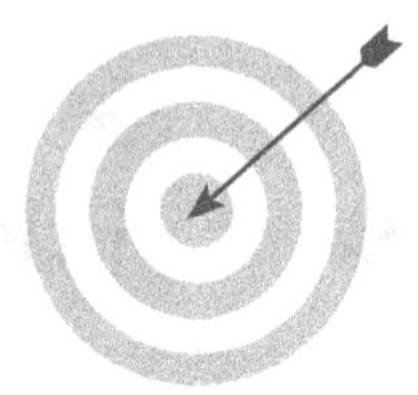

86

Start a Blog

A weblog, or 'blog' as it is more commonly referred to, is a platform where a writer or a group of writers share their views on a particular subject.

Blogging about your PSM I experience is a great way to help others who are looking to follow in your footsteps. You should try to write your blog post as soon as possible after passing the assessment, whilst it's still fresh in your memory.

How to write a blog post in five easy steps

Step 1 - Plan your blog post by choosing a topic, creating an outline, conducting research, and checking facts.

Step 2 - Craft a headline that is both informative and will capture readers' attention.

Step 3 - Write your post, either writing a draft in a single session or gradually working on parts of it.

Step 4 - Use images to enhance your post, improve its flow, add humour, and explain complex topics.

Step 5 - Edit your blog post. Make sure to avoid repetition, read your post aloud to check its flow, have someone else read it and provide feedback, keep sentences and paragraphs short, don't be a perfectionist, don't be afraid to cut out text or change things at last minute.

87

Update Your LinkedIn

You've worked hard and passed the PSM I, so now is the time to tell the world that you're a certified Professional Scrum Master!

Share your PSM I on LinkedIn

Adding your Scrum.org certification details to LinkedIn is easy enough. To add your certification, simply click on 'add certifications' when editing your LinkedIn profile. Follow the instructions to copy and paste your Certificate information to your LinkedIn profile.

Scrum.org's certificates are not numbered, but if you wish to use a License Number, they recommend you use your Scrum.org member ID. You can find this by logging into your account on Scrum.org, navigating to 'my profile' and then copying the number in the URL after the last backslash. For example: http://www.scrum.org/user/xxxx. The 'xxxx' would be your member ID.

This will then be viewable under the 'Accomplishments' section of your LinkedIn profile.

88

Share your PSM I Achievement in a New Post

Create a new LinkedIn post that focusses on your takeaways from passing, and what you are proud of accomplishing, and the impact that it is having on your career.

If you attended a PSM I training course, be sure to tag your PST in the post, so they will see it and help you celebrate. By adding tags (for example #professionalscrummaster, #Scrum.org) you are increasing the chances of your post reaching more people, both inside and outside of your professional network.

One success can often lead to another, so maximise the exposure of your recent accomplishment. This practice has been known to transform people's careers, creating opportunities for them to move upwards and onto the next level.

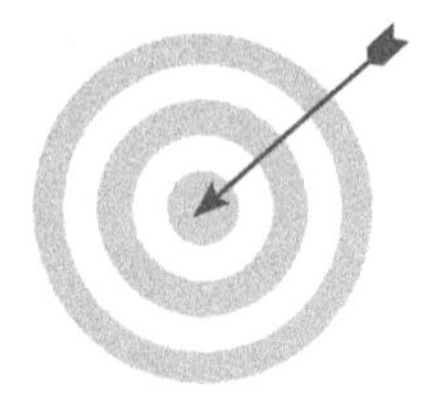

89

Share PSM I Success on the Scrum.org Forum

It's easy to pass the assessment and quickly move onto your next goal or challenge, but remember: by sharing your PSM I success story you can provide inspiration and motivation to others who are struggling to achieve the same.

Scrum.org's forum is a great way for you to share your experience of passing the PSM I assessment. Future PSM I candidates value your feedback and are counting on you to share your story so that they too, can adopt some of your success strategies.

In helping others, you help yourself

There is a Chinese saying that goes: 'If you want happiness for an hour, take a nap. If you want happiness for a day, go fishing. If you want happiness for a year, inherit a fortune. If you want happiness for a lifetime, help somebody.'

There is a plethora of information available in books and on the internet to prove that helping others is actually beneficial for your own mental health and well-being.

Scrum.org is always seeking to develop their certifications, so your feedback will be valuable in helping them improve their assessment offerings.

PSM I Public Listing with Scrum.org

Once you've received your email from Scrum.org confirming that you've been awarded your designation as a certified PSM I, your name will appear on the Scrum.org website under the 'Certification List' section.

If you have earned your PSM I certification but are unable to find your name on the list of certification holders, contact support@scrum.org for assistance.

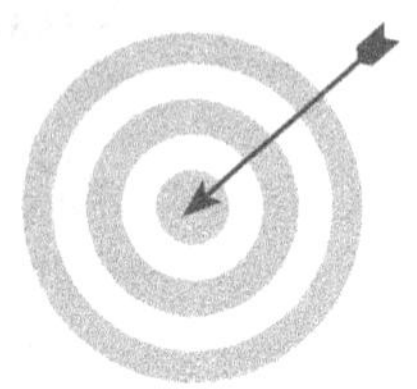

90

Set Your Next Professional Goal

Just like life goals, career goals are essential to professional development; there can be no growth without goals. Education never ends and nor should it. Even if you're a CEO or working full-time in your dream career, there is always room for growth and improved knowledge, especially in the realm of professional certifications.

PSM II

You may be considering taking the PSM II as the next step in your professional development. Having demonstrated a fundamental understanding of Scrum mastery, you may feel you are ready to prove your underlying knowledge of Scrum principles and demonstrate that you can apply these in the real world.

While the PSM I assessment is mostly about the basics and theory of the Scrum framework, mixed with general questions to test your Agile mindset, PSM II has a much wider set of topics, including Teaching, Organisational Design and Structure, Product Vision and Evidence Based Management.

Career goals are essential for

- Keeping yourself passionate and invigorated about your career;
- Finding out if it's time for a job change;
- Learning more about yourself as a person, and
- Becoming multi-skilled and/or perfecting your craft.

The first step is to generate a list of goals to choose from. Before you decide what to pursue, list all the possibilities. Goal setting is your opportunity to write your own story... but give yourself permission to think big! Practicality is not your friend at this stage. Leave all notions of 'should' or what 'makes sense' aside for now. These are the steps I followed in order to write this book!

PROFESSIONAL CERTIFICATION

PROFESSIONAL SCRUM MASTER I

Emma Key

has demonstrated a fundamental level of Scrum mastery, including the concepts of applying Scrum, and proven an understanding of Scrum as described in the Scrum Guide. This individual has also demonstrated a consistent use of terminology and approach to Scrum.

In recognition of this achievement, Scrum.org is pleased to award this certification.

Ken Schwaber, founder Scrum.org

February 1, 2016
Certification Date

Scrum.org PSM I

https://scrum.org/certificates/140520

www.ingramcontent.com/pod-product-compliance
Lightning Source LLC
Chambersburg PA
CBHW070356270326
41926CB00014B/2576

* 9 7 8 0 6 4 8 9 9 0 8 0 2 *